NOTES IN TROAS

ADENIYI AYENI

ISBN 978-1-68526-351-5 (Paperback)
ISBN 978-1-68526-352-2 (Digital)

Copyright © 2023 Adeniyi Ayeni
All rights reserved
First Edition

All rights reserved. No part of this publication may be reproduced, distributed, or transmitted in any form or by any means, including photocopying, recording, or other electronic or mechanical methods without the prior written permission of the publisher. For permission requests, solicit the publisher via the address below.

Covenant Books
11661 Hwy 707
Murrells Inlet, SC 29576
www.covenantbooks.com

10/06/2019
MY MIND AND BRAIN

These are working together for God.

> And God saw that the wickedness of man was great in the earth, and that every imagination of the thoughts of his heart was only evil continually. (Genesis 6:5)

> And be not conformed to this world; but be ye transformed by the renewing of your mind that ye may prove what is that good, and acceptable, and perfect, will of God. (Romans 12:2)

This morning in our Bible study, which is a very important part of the service, we talked about hypocrisy. There is a definition to it but—by my interpretation of what it is—if you said you believe in Jesus Christ and you do what is contrary to His commandments, you are definitely a liar (John 14:15).

You cannot deceive God! If you want to walk with Him, you have to be on His side (Amos 3:3). There's a standard when it comes to kingdom's things lukewarmness is not a given. You cannot confess what you don't possess. Many people have crosses on their chests but no Christ in their lives. If your friends of a lifetime cannot differentiate your lifestyle since you became born again, you still do the same stuff you did in the past, then you are not in Christ but in crisis. It is not a thousand but the number of people that are ready to journey to heaven. Determination is key to setting aside all those filthy things. Challenges come your way if truly you are a Christian. There are challenges that happen to prove our faith (John 16:33). But some men of little faith begin to fidget and faint during their trying times.

> If you faint in the day of adversity, thy strength is small. (Proverbs 24:10)

Take for instance the three Hebrew boys, Shadrach, Meshach, and Abednego. They made up their minds to follow God. They were unwavering in their decision to serve the one and only true God (Daniel 3). Your aura should portray the peace of *God* which qualifies you for His benefits. The acts of indecent dressing, filthy works, and drinking are the things that draw people to sin and take them far from God. Maybe part of the reasons God will not allow drunks in His kingdom is that they might start picking fights with God if there are no provisions for beer and gin in new heaven. Let people rethink actions and inactions. The things you do that do not glorify the name of the Lord should be done away with.

Today we are addressing the issue of mind and brain. The brain is one of the largest and most complex organs in the human body. It is made up of more than one hundred billion nerves that communicate in trillions of connections. The brain is the functional part of the body controlling the physical structure. the frontal lobes are responsible for problem solving, judgment, and motor function. The parietal lobes manage sensation, handwriting, and body position. The temporal lobes are involved with memory and hearing. And the occipital lobes contain the brain's visual processing system.

Why did I break it down? I want you to know how crucial and important our brain is. So at the point of insanity, all human dignity is eroded because the brain has lost all its functions. The brain controls every part of the body. The mind is the process by which the brain works. The spiritual side is very interesting. God knows whatever is going on in our minds. We conceive an idea in our minds, and *God* helps us actualize it.

> The plans of the heart belong to man, but the answer of the tongue is from the Lord. (Proverbs 16:1)

When we are in our thought process, we think of ways to work through some challenges or life issues without knowing God is actually working behind the scenes to actualize our dreams.

In Genesis 11:4, it makes us realize that the people were still in their thought process to come together to build the tower. They had not started laying the bricks. It was all in their imagination.

> And they said, Go to, let us build us a city and a tower, whose top may reach unto heaven; and let us make us a name; lest we be scattered abroad upon the face of the whole earth. (Genesis 11:4)

At that point, God came down to look at the city. To God it was already real. Physically, it wasn't; but to God, it was already built. So he had to come down to see.

> And the Lord came down to see the city and the tower, which the children of men builded. (Genesis 11:5)

In the physical world, it wasn't real (imagination) (verse 6); but to God, it was already actualized.

The moment you think about anything, it becomes real to *God*. They already built it in their minds, so it's settled. Procrastination is the work of the devil to delay humans from actualizing their God-given destiny. The moment you conceive an idea, the thought of a good deed in line with the will of God for your life, God already sent angels to dispatch the resources to help realize your thoughts. Not that there won't be obstacles that can make someone start fidgeting but, the angel of the Lord has been sent to help you. So start seeing yourself as a future employer of labor. Sit down and think yourself out of the box. If your boss likes you, it's because he's using you. He's not looking out for you just because he loves you. He's only using you for cheap. Address your imagination. Sit down and think big. Keep at it, either you fail or rise (Genesis 11:6).

The major problem confronting us is the *how* factor, which is really God's to solve, not for us to sit down and complain. Behind the obstacles on our way is the glory of God. Without the Red Sea, there won't be Canaan land. Without Goliath, David won't be recognized. Some obstacles are stepping stones to glory. At some point, God will surely come through.

Your mind and brain are very important. Guide your jealousy and focus on *God*.

> Keep thy heart with all diligence for out of it are
> the issues of life. (Proverbs 4:23)

Among the issues you must consider are discipline and self-control. We must be disciplined in our actions and exercise some self-control. If we can imagine it in our mind and put ourselves together in prayers, that *how* comes to play from our Creator. If you can conceive a good idea, God can deliver it. Just trust in Him.

Your mind and brain cannot work perfectly with *God* until you are born again. If you want to start a relationship with the Lord *Jesus Christ* or you have one time or the other given your life, but you derailed, you can pray this prayer:

> Lord Jesus, Lord Jesus, Lord Jesus,
> I confess all my sins and repent of them.
> I accept you as my Savior.
> I will follow you as my Lord.
> Thank you for saving me. Amen.

10/13/2019
FEAR NOT

> But now thus says the Lord, He who created you, o Jacob, He who formed you, o Israel: "Fear not, for I have redeemed you; I have called you by name, you are mine. (Isaiah 43:1)

The Lord knows all we were meant to achieve on earth. He is saying to fear not, which appears 365 times in the Bible. It means to use one each day. When you fear, a license is given to the devil to work on the person's behalf. Circumstances and situations that will make us fearful will come. Whirlwinds will come, but the spirit of God is telling us not to fear. Hallelujah! Any problem that comes our way is to make us glorify the name of the Lord. When you exercise faith, you are asking God to get involved in your issues. But when you exercise fear, you are giving the devil permission to get involved. Isaiah 43 verse 2 says, "When you pass through the waters, I will be with you; And through the rivers, they shall not overwhelm you; When you walk through fire you shall not be burned, And the flame shall not consume you." When you find yourself in a dilemma at a crossroad, so confused that you have nowhere to go, God says, "Do not fear." Always put one very important factor: *God* factor. This phrase makes you unique and different from others. Rivers will overflow. Storms of life will rage. But because your foundation is on the rock of ages, it will end in praise. *God* says that when you walk through the fire, it will not burn you because you have *Him*. He's got your back always. Take for instance the analogy of gold. As shiny as it is, it's due to the fact that it passed through the fiery furnace. For you to be successful in life to carry that value, you got to be tested and trusted. God says that the fire will not burn us. After the test, the glory of God will outshine all the sorrows and end in praise.

10/20/2019
SOUND OF ABUNDANCE OF BLESSINGS

> Blessed is the man that trusted in the Lord and whose hope the lord is, For He shall be as a tree planted by the waters, and that spread out her roots by the river, and shall not see when heat comes, but her leaf shall be green and shall not be careful in the year of drought, neither shall cease from yielding fruit. (Jeremiah 17:7–8)

Brethren, every man looks up to God. He does not look up to no man.

> The eyes of all wait upon thee; and thou givest them their meat in due season. (Psalm 145:15)

If God is praised, every man ought to be happy.

> You will show me the path of life; in your presence is fullness of joy; in your right hand there are pleasure forever. (Psalm 16:11 AMP)

God sat on the platform of nothing, and He brought something out of nothing (Genesis 1:1).

Men's opinion is irrelevant once you have God's approval. If *God* is for me, who can be against me? I have angels standing in for me. Mercy and grace are speaking loud in our lives. When God sanctions a thing, the totality of heaven swings into action. It is only a fool that doubts proof because the result justifies the means.

Prosperity in the kingdom of God is not an achievement; it is an entrustment. God is the owner of everything on earth, but He entrusted it in your care for the benefit of *His* kingdom and mankind.

> If therefore you have not been faithful in the unrighteous mammon, who will commit to your *trust* the true riches. (Luke 16:11)

Abundance is specifically mentioned in the Bible as something God offers to those who trust in Him. God provides abundant life to those who seek *Him* and His righteousness first. That is everything needed to sustain your life. This is not limited to money alone but the blessings include protection and peace. God's blessings are meant to protect us, guide us to the path of righteousness, and give us hope.

Elijah confronted the prophet of Baal, and God confirmed his presence. The confrontation starts in 1 Kings 18:16–18. Ahab went to meet Elijah and said to him that he was the troubler of Israel, but Elijah replied to him, "I have not trouble Israel but you and your father's house because you have abandoned the commandment of the Lord and followed the Baals."

You can serve any gods you want, but at some point, God will meet you at a very high altitude where you have no choice but to acknowledge *Him* as your Lord and personal Savior.

Elijah suggested that two bulls be given to them, one to the prophets of Baal and one to him. He said, "Choose one bull for yourselves [450 prophets of Baal and 400 prophets of Asherah] and cut it in pieces and lay it on the wood but put no fire to it, and I will prepare the other bull and lay it on the wood and put no fire on it. And you call upon the name of your god, and I will call upon the name of the Lord and the God who answers by fire. He is God." And all the people answered, "Yes, it is well spoken."

First Kings 18:25–26 shows that the prophets of Baal prepared the bull and set it on the wood and called the name of their god from morning to noon, saying "O Baal, answer us!" But there was no voice, and no one answered. And so they tried till evening, all to no avail.

Then Elijah said to all the people, "Come near to me," and he repaired the altar of the Lord that had been thrown down. He also made a trench about the altar as great as would contain two seahs of seed, put the wood in order, cut the bull in pieces, laid it on the wood, and asked the people to fill four jars with water and pour it on the burnt offering and on the wood. This was repeated three times. Elijah said, "O Lord God of Abraham, Isaac, and Israel, let it be known this day that you are God in Israel and that I am your servant." Immediately, fire of the Lord fell and consumed the burnt offering, the wood, stones, and dust and licked up the water.

> And Elijah said to Ahab, "Go up, eat and drink,
> for there is a sound of the rushing of rain."
> (1 Kings 18:41)

God sent down an abundance of rain to quench the three and half years of drought and famine.

God brought you to his sanctuary to resharpen your life. Jesus declared to us that He came so that we may have life and have it in abundance. The only thing that can give you your inheritance amongst those that are sanctified is the word of God because, out of the word, we were made. God had already told Elijah that he should show himself to Ahab and *He* would send rain (1 kings 18:1). So all the confidence Elijah was showing was based on the promise of God to send rain.

The word of God is potent enough to produce an abundance of everything we may stand in need (Psalm 107:20), including healing and deliverance.

Mary told the people at the marriage feast when they ran out of supply, "Whatever He says unto you, do it" (John 2:5).

When the crowd ran out of food in the wilderness, His word was to multiply a little boy's lunch. Jesus said that they did not need to go away, and therefore the disciples were to give them something to eat. they said that they only had five loaves and two fishes, which Jesus asked to be brought to Him. Jesus directed the people to sit down in groups on the grass, and He prayed and gave the food back to the disciples to be distributed to the crowd. After all was said and done, twelve baskets were left over after five thousand men had eaten, excluding women and children, which normally constitute the highest number in any gathering (Matthew 14:13–21).

If a situation that is not according to your expectation/plan now does not mean it can't change. There will be light at the end of the tunnel. With God, nothing is impossible.

To live in abundance, consider the following:

1. Have an abundant mentality. (If you want to be a star, you must act like one.)
2. Be grateful. Value what you have.
3. Smile.
4. Start each day right.
5. Get ready for an impromptu opportunity. (It is better to prepare for an opportunity and not get one than to get one and not be prepared for it.)
6. Make the most out of every opportunity.
7. Build and maintain healthy relationships.

How to experience/attract abundance

1. You must submit to God so He can help you.
    Job 22:21–29; 1 Kings 18:1 Genuine prophets carry the word of God with them wherever they go (Jeremiah 3:15) if a pastor is not wordful, then he is not worthy.
2. Give.
    Give yourself to Jesus before you give anything (2 Corinthians 8:15). Your capacity to give determines the level of blessings allocated to you.

3. You must have faith.
   Anybody can claim to know *God*, but it actually matters when God knows you (Genesis 18: 19; 2 Timothy 2:19).

It is not branded by church or denomination, which also is not a requirement or visa to heaven. It is your heart that really matters to God. Brethren, depart from iniquity. Let your heart be pure. You are not useful until God recognizes you as a candidate for His kingdom. You are not a vessel unto honor until you are genuinely born again. Carry the gospel with you wherever you go. Bear the mark of the cross, and you shall see the glory of God. Amen!

10/27/2019
THE BLESSINGS OF HARVEST

According to Charles Jones, five years from today, you will be the same person you were with the exception of the books you read and the company you keep.

The company you keep determines the future you see.

> He that walk with wise men shall be wise; but a companion of fools shall be destroyed. (Proverbs 13:20)

God is a God of secret.

> The secret things belong unto the Lord our God; but those things which are revealed belong unto us and to our children forever, that we may do all the words of the law. (Deuteronomy 29:29)

The secret things God revealed to you determine the future already prepared for you.

> The secret of the Lord is with them that fear Him; and He will show them His covenant. (Psalm 25:14)

If God can show you the future, it is because he already revealed the secret beforehand. If *God* can show you the way, there's no distraction again.

Harvest is used in the Bible to refer to two different occasions: (1) the gathering of things planted, a natural time of reaping in joy what has been sown and produced during the year, and (2) the rescuing of the remains of Israel and the resurrection of believers from the earth.

My sermon today is based on the first one. The Lord commanded the children of Israel to celebrate the festival of harvest twice in the year. First is the firstfruits of the crops sown at the beginning of the year, and the second is the ingathering of all the crops at the end of the year.

> And the feast of harvest, the firstfruits of thy labours, which thou hast sown in the field and the feast of ingathering, which is in the end of the year, when thou has gathered in thy labours out of the field. (Exodus 23:16)

God does not need our crops or our money. What God is really looking for is to be first in all things and our attitude of gratitude in recognition of His provision for all living. No one can totally provide everything he needs for himself. All eyes are looking unto God for provision, and the desire of every creature is satisfied by the Lord.

> The eyes of all wait upon thee; and thou givest them their meat in due season. Thou openest thine hand, and satisfies the desire of every living thing. (Psalm 145:15–16)

The heart of the giver is much more important to God more than the quality or quantity of the item given.

Jesus Christ sat opposite the treasury and observed how the crowd put money into the treasure. Many rich people put in large sums, and many wealthy put in substantial amounts of money. But there came a poor widow. She put in two small coins, like two cents. Jesus, calling His disciple to himself, said to them, "This poor widow puts in more than all the other contributors to the treasure, for they have all contributed from their surplus wealth. But she, from her poverty, has contributed all she had, her whole livelihood" (Mark 12:41–44; Luke 21:1–4).

Benefit of giving

1. It serves as our worship to God (Psalm 116:12, 14, 8; Ecclesiastes 5:1–7; Proverbs 20:27; Matthew 6:21).
2. We please God with our giving (Philippians 4:18; 2 Corinthians 9:7).
3. Our giving allows God to act on our behalf (Lamentations 3:25, Romans 8:28, Isaiah 40:29–31).
4. God uses our giving to multiply our blessing (Luke 6:38).

What you keep is all you have. What you give is what God multiplies.

If you plant a seed in good ground, you are going to get a harvest from that seed. In fact, "Do not be deceived: God cannot be mocked. A man reaps what he sows" (Galatians 6:7). If you read on in the context, Apostle Paul said that if you sow seeds of unrighteousness, if you do wicked things, you are going to have wicked responses to what you do. You will reap what you sow or even reap more than you sow. When you plant a seed in good ground, you will reap more than you sow.

Jesus said, "And everyone who has left houses or brothers or sisters or father or mother or children or fields for my sake will receive a hundred times as much and will inherit eternal life" (Matthew 19:29).

If you lay down your life for Christ, you will receive far more than you have given. Jesus talked about this principle in Matthew 13. He said a sower went out to sow some seeds. He was just throwing seeds out, and they fell along different places, and some of them returned a thirtyfold, some a sixtyfold. And those planted in really good soil returned a hundredfold.

In the Christian race, our teacher is the Holy Spirit. Once we follow Him, we won't miss out on the blessings of the harvest. Many commit their time to the kingdom business. They also cannot miss out.

Deuteronomy 28:1–2 states, "And it shall come to pass, if thou shalt hearken diligently unto the voice of the lord thy God, to observe and to do all His commandment which I command thee this day, that the lord thy God shall set thee on high above all nations of the earth. And all these blessings shall come on thee and overtake thee if thou shall hearken unto the voice of the lord thy God." This is the voice of Moses instructing the Israelites, reminding them to observe all the commandments of God. One of the things God commanded us to do is the harvest (Matthew 6:33). The blessings of the harvest are coming upon us according to the promises of God. All you need to do is get ready to receive it in your health, finances, marriages, and academics.

We did what God commanded us to do. It is time to wait for his blessings (Exodus 23v25). Our major requirement is to serve the Lord. The blessings our Lord Jesus Christ promised to bestow upon us for the harvest cannot be compared to any other thing in this world. All the beautiful promises of Christ will manifest in our lives in the name of Jesus. (Amen!) Prepare your barn (house) because the blessings of God will manifest in your life so much so that people will see you and want to serve your God.

11/03/2019
PATIENCE

Genesis 39 states that Joseph was a servant, a slave in Potiphar's house. He was a conqueror over sexual immorality. God prospered him despite his low status. His industrialism became apparent, hence his attractiveness to his master and household. His brothers stripped him of his clothes of many colors but could not strip him of his glory.

> Whoever is in Christ is a new creature. (2 Corinthians 5:17)

Eccl 3:14 states that anything that belongs to God can never be tampered with. When you are going on an appointment, *He* lives in you so He is on that mission with you. Patience is defined as a person's ability to wait through a tedious situation, waiting for God to do what He has promised (1 Peter 1:6). While acting it, there's no way you can get what you want from God without being patient. Hurry does not apply to God because His actions are based on time and purpose. *He* already purported whatever He does in His heart. The birth of Jesus had been prophesied since the Old Testament, which is an indication that, if you want to walk with God, you have to be patient. Believers have to be calm in the face of challenges. The key word is the ability to wait, meaning you are waiting on someone (God) for something. Ecclesiastes 3:1 emphasizes that there is time for everything under the sun. When it is time for God, He will definitely act. There's always a wait time, which is a time between a request and answer, a time between a vision and accomplishment.

The reason Christians face challenges is that we try to eradicate our wait time. That is why Christians had to wait for the coming of our Lord Jesus Christ since the prophecies came concerning Him in the Old Testament. For every Christian, there is a wait time. You cannot fast-forward it. People who cannot endure run from pillar to post, getting involved in things that are ungodly, because they are in too much of a hurry. Habakkuk 2:3 states, "The vision is yet for an appointed time." This is God speaking to us in this context. God already gave His prophet the vision ahead of time, but there's an appointed time set for the vision to come to actualization because *He* does His work ahead of time—time to plan, to plant, to wait, and then germinate. That is why it is always good for Christians to wait on the Lord. God will help us to wait for Him in Jesus's name. Why is waiting time important? A wait time symbolizes a challenging period. The devil will try to bring distractions that will make our hearts waver, not to be able to wait on *His* promises. The story of Joseph that we talked briefly about earlier today at the beginning of this sermon, when his battle started, it actually started from his family (brothers) before he even got to Potiphar where his wife tried seducing him, which led to his imprisonment. While in prison, he encountered the king's butler and servant who forgot him for years. But all through his ordeal, he waited.

Think about how far Joseph had gone (thirteen years) from the time God gave him the vision till the time of fulfillment. Even Abraham, when I studied the man critically, the fact that he waited twenty-five years did not bother me. I was bothered in Genesis 15:1 where he challenged God that how long, oh Lord, would he go childless. It can really get to that point in a Christian journey. But the point is for us to be patient! Distractions, doubts, and fears creep in to take you away from what you are expecting from God. Psalm 121 is where King David said he would lift up his eyes to the Lord. That is when you lift up your eyes to God. You will be blind to distractions around you. I will keep looking up to God because *He* promised that He would fulfill that which He said He would. *He* said to ask, and He will give (Hebrews 12:2–3). The best way to learn to build our faith in waiting for the Lord is to look up to God. When Jesus came to the world, He endured a lot of humiliation from the scribes, Pharisees, all of them; but He endured. I asked myself why He had to go through all these. The fact is that all the challenges He faced were His wait time. God already told Him the end result of His challenges; but on His part, He had to work on it. Our solution is to pray and constantly remind *Him* of His promises.

> Followers of those who through faith and patience. (Hebrews 6:12–15)

Faith alone cannot work because you already believe He can do that which He promised you. But he is not in a rush, so we cannot expect *Him* to turn into a magician because of a particular issue. So while we are waiting, He's working behind the scene.

Patience (inherit the promises)

> And let us run with patience the race set before us. (Hebrews 12:1–2)

Let us run our various races with patience because people will challenge our faith. People will create fears in your mind. But at the set time from God, He will attend to our cases. *He* works with patient people. A lot of people lost their lives, marriages, homes, finances, social status just because they are expecting God to perform some kind of magic on their issues. God is not a magician. As I had said earlier, *He* does His work gradually and according to *His* timing and purpose. The more reason it is easy for fake prophets to exploit Christians is that some are gullible enough to believe anything and also want quick solutions to their problems. It is important for Christians to know the kind of God they serve before false prophets start playing upon their intelligence. If God should open our eyes, we will see a whole lot of evil going on in the world today. I pray, in the name above all names, none of us will fall into their evil traps in Jesus's name. Amen! After doing the will of God, answers don't come immediately. You need patience received from God. For instance, when you are looking up to God for a particular thing, people tend to brand you. But these challenges actually build our trust in God more during our wait time (Galatians 5:22). I want to encourage us to live a life worthy of emulation in the matters of the kingdom of God. There is time for revelation, preparations, planning, and then manifestation. The Bible says that those that wait on the Lord shall renew their strength. Let us pray to God that we shall not fall prey to the devil's antics during our wait time.

11/8/2019
DIVINE WISDOM

There are four types of wisdom according to James 3:15. Earthly, sensual devillish and verse 17 talked about wisdom from above. Proverbs 8—Earthly Wisdom. Earthly wisdom or common knowledge. When you give birth to a baby, you don't have to teach the baby some stuff like eating, smiling, or even crying, unlike sensual wisdom, which is what you major in school. It's a given, if and when you are educated. For example, doctors or surgeons work on humans and treat them. Or take for instance the sensual knowledge behind the aircraft that flies in the air with over two hundred people and their baggage. God imparted the engineers to better a lot of humans. Then again, there is the diabolical wisdom used by the evil ones to do evil. It's also the wisdom of God manipulated in the wrong way. Out of all these, there's the divine wisdom, the wisdom of God. When *He* is speaking over your situation, authority speaks. Proverbs 8:32 shows the way and moment it comes over life. When Abraham was in Ur of the Chaldeans. Again, when the Israelites where in the Red Sea, God made a dry road for them to pass through right in the bottom of the sea. This is the wisdom of God! When you knock on the door, it opens for you through prayers. You cannot get it in education or the classroom. The only way to access divine wisdom is to be a friend of *God*. Heed His instructions. John 1v3: states, "In *Him* is light, darkness cannot comprehend." This means the powers and principalities of this world will have no dominion over you. Anything you touch will turn to gold. I see that happening in our lives in the mighty name of Jesus! Proverbs 8:36 states that sin does not affect God. When you sin, you block *Him* out of your life. You no longer have access to Him unless you repent. You cannot be comfortable with God and also comfortable with sin. Verse 34 highlights obedience to the voice of God. When you obey the voice of God, He will grant you His wisdom (Luke 16:11). Prosperity in the kingdom is not an accomplishment; it's an entrustment. There's no help coming from anywhere except God. Psalm 1:1 says that whatever you do shall prosper because you are endowed with *His* wisdom. Things around you begin to be done perfectly. Many times, those things we see as problems are not to God. They are sometimes a form of our step-up to glory when you have wisdom from above (Colossians 3:1). Heaven will be our priority. God wants to be first in our lives. *He* doesn't want to be just there. What differentiates Solomon from every other king on earth was the wisdom God gave him, but his disobedience lured him away from the presence of God by following other gods, seeking the face of mediums, etc. May we not lose our place in glory in Jesus's name. Amen!

11/10/2019
OPERATING ON GOD'S MERCY

> It is of the Lord's mercies that we are not consumed because His compassion fails not. (Lamentations 3:22)

God's grace is immeasurable. His mercy is inexhaustible. His peace is inexpressible.

> Justice and judgment are the habitation of thy throne; mercy and truth shall go before thy face. (Psalm 89:14)

> The lord is gracious, and full of compassion; slow to anger and of great mercy. The lord is good to all; and His tender mercies are over all His works. (Psalm 145:8–9)

What is mercy?

It is the attribute of God, which is as a result and effect of His goodness.

I would like to start today's sermon by glorifying the name of the Lord. We serve an awesome God who doesn't consult our past to determine our future. He knows all things and can do all things. The Lord makes promises and has the power to fulfill them. He is the ancient of days. He began before the beginning of creation when there was nothing on the surface of this world. He stepped out of Himself, stood on the pinnacle of nothing, and used the invisible material to create something visible. He made a commandment to the sea where they should not pass. He creates the visible from the invisible. He gives power to the waters, the wind. He is the almighty, all knowing, all sufficient. That God is visiting us again today in Jesus's name.

Whenever I realize the anointing of God over my life, the authority of heaven backing me up, there's no mountain that I cannot surmount because *He* has all the power and authority. I see the power of God manifesting and working in your favor today in the name of Jesus!

Brethren, listen to me and listen well. The word of God will never come down from heaven and return to Him void unless it fulfills that which its purpose to do. God does not need you for anything, but you need God for everything to eat, breathe, walk, work, sleep, and wake up—just about anything. Listen, brethren, your situation is far better than millions out there. There are some people whose destiny has been truncated by insanity. Their reasoning has been derailed in the instance of madness where all dignity is gone and the value lost. God did not allow all these challenges in your life.

I am challenging your faith right now. Whatever you might be asking from God is secondary because he has taken care of the first thing (being alive). All other things are additions. At the point of death, nobody seeks marriage, money, education, etc. God has favored us. He did not allow all these evils to befall us. We are on the top of the ground, not under the ground. And because we are on the surface, for the mere fact that you are still walking, still living under His grace, God has not closed our case. There is still time for Him to advance us, bless us, open closed doors, and do wonders in our lives. I see God performing wonders in our lives in Jesus's name.

Today I will be talking about what I call operating on God's mercy. This is the situation where you are no longer operating in the class of mere men, but you are operating on divine strength. That's the level I expect you to get to in the Lord where His grace is immeasurable. His peace is inexpressible. His mercy has no limit. It can bring provisions where there's none, bring forth children where there's none, and increase your financial ability when you are down. His grace is unmatchable.

Mercy is an attribute of the effectiveness of God's goodness. He does not only give mercy, He Himself is merciful.

> Bless the lord, o my soul and all that is within me bless his holy name Bless the lord o my soul and forget not all his benefits; Who forgiveth all thine iniquities; who healeth all thy diseases Who redeemeth thy life from destruction; who crowneth thee with lovingkindness and tender mercies Who satisfieth thy mouth with good things so that thy youth is renewed like the eagle; The lord executes righteousness and judgment for all that are oppressed; He made known his ways unto Moses and his acts unto the children of Israel; the lord is merciful and gracious, slow to anger and plenteous in mercy. (Psalm 103:1–8)

I see that mercy engulfing us today in the name of Jesus!

Psalm 102:13, says that there's always a set time for the favor of God to manifest in your life. There's a set time for God to promote you, to give you that thing that you think is impossible. I am here today to announce to you that your set time for mercy has come in the mighty name of Jesus. Do I have an evangelist in the house?

Mercy is a blessing—that is, an act of divine compassion, "for God so loved the world that He gave His only begotten son" out of His love and benevolence. He set Himself outside of Himself to rescue the world. And then I say that he who has no love has no benefit of mercy because God is love who expresses His mercy as part of His attribute. What is mercy? It is the act of sparing you from the punishment you deserve. What is grace? It is God giving you what you don't deserve, what you cannot ordinarily get by your human effort. There's a way God redeems time through mercy. When the mercy of God is in place, He redeems time for you. All the time you thought you had lost, He brings them all together to favor you, like a woman looking up to God for the fruit of the womb who got answers to her prayers at a very old age. God gave her triplets to make up for all the years she lost. What you cannot achieve ordinarily, grace brought it hither. Many of us despite all the things we thought we should have achieved in life, God can raise our children to achieve these things by redeeming the time for us through mercy. Grace brought you to the house of God, but mercy preserves you. I see that mercy working for you in the name of Jesus!

It's not always good for Christians to say at the verge of success that the devil comes to crumble what they had been gathering. No! You are unmolestable. In God's kingdom, we are seated with Christ far above the principalities and powers that be, above their imaginations and realm of Satan. That's why it is not always good for Christians to confess negative things to their situations. No! If you are a genuine Christian, you are seated with Christ. We cannot be embarrassed. The mercy of God will empower you to achieve what you had been struggling to achieve in forty years in just four days.

The mountain you cannot climb. When the mercy of God is with you, He sets you far above the pinnacle, and you become a surprise and marvel to all. Hallelujah to the Son of the living God!

Some time ago, I gave a sermon on an eighteen-year-old boy who gave his life after the message. He said he was touched by the message. He said he had a power given to him by his grandfather. I told him there's *one* greater than all these powers on earth. He asked where the power was at, and I told him that *Jesus* is the only true power (Psalm 62–11) that if he wants the power of God, he has to let go of all the evil power in his possession. He repented and gave them all up. I prayed for him and led him to Jesus. Brethren, I want to admonish you today to go out into the world and walk with the consciousness of Christ and His mercy over your life.

In whatever area you are looking up to God, know that you are not alone. The mercy of God is a factor that will make our cases and situations unique and different. Those of you in businesses, students, I want you to know that the mercy of God is with you. What stopped others cannot stop you because the spoken word of God has authority over your situation or thoughts. That's why it is good to speak out positivity. When the mercy of God is in your life, be rest assured that you are rich. Today is just another new beginning. God is working out signs and wonders to take you where you want to be. Don't judge your life by today's situation. Life is in phases. Don't allow your life to be defined by today's phase. No! The Bible says, do not despise the time of your small beginnings (Zechariah 4:10), which indicates things might be a little tough from the start. Preparation for glory is in phases. God is preparing you. Jesus had to stay in the wilderness. Fasting and praying for forty days and nights—that was his wilderness time. Most of us are in our wilderness time right now (Luke 1:80), but know fully well that our time of glory and showing off is at hand in the name of Jesus! He has promises for us that we shall be comfortable. He will bless you front, back, right, and center.

What about healing when He made a promise for us in 1 Peter 2:24 that by His stripes we are healed? There's no sickness that can remain with you forever without the mercy of God stepping in to heal it. Don't nurture sickness. Don't celebrate poverty. Don't tell God how big your problem is. Rather, tell your problem how big your God is. I told you in this church that when you are working for an organization, you are an asset to them. Let them know they have the privilege of having you because God is blessing them through you. Don't you know what God said concerning Joseph? That because he is in the house of Potiphar, God blessed him this is the mercy of God showing up for you at work. You have to walk as if you carry the undeniable mercy of God. Paul the apostle, who wrote two-thirds of the New Testament, said, "I'm what I am by His grace not by my knowledge, smartness, education. And I can do all things through Christ that strengthens me." Your case is different because you carry the authority and anointing of Christ that cannot be denied.

Don't walk as if you are under a heavy burden or struggling with life. No! Walk shoulder high with Christ in you. I'm not talking about being arrogant. I want you to walk as if you carry Christ, and there's no door you knock that the mercy of Christ will not open for you.

What are the requirements to walk at the mercy of God?

1 Obedience to the word of God is required as per the Bible standard. It is the degree of your compliance to the instruction of God that determines prosperity and your mercy placement. When your obedience to His instructions is high, God will place you high (Job 36:11). You cannot be in this church and be comfortable with sin no matter what. Obedience to the word of God is a demand and a must. If you want to spend your years in fortune and prosperity, obey *Him*! Obedience to the word of God will deliver your fortune to you among those that are sanctified. He will deliver your inheritance to you. It is not by labor but by favor. It is not by might but by the Spirit who is performing wonders. Until you do what is required, what is desired may not be delivered. Praise the Lord (2 Chronicles 20:20). The wind will blow against you. Rain will beat against you but, your foundation is in Christ. Circumstances and conditions will come, but they will not overcome you. That is the difference between you and an unbeliever, regardless of whatever obstacle you might have encountered. If you are serving God faithfully, you will always have cause to give testimony. Hebrew 6:10; Deuteronomy 28:1 states that if you find yourself in a difficult situation today, it might be due to your failure to comply with the instructions of God. But we are blessed because we can always retrace our steps to know where we faulted. Temptations will come our way, but the ability to say no is what God is waiting for to lift you up. I know, beyond a shadow of doubt, this year, God is lifting you up in the mighty name of Jesus.

2 Another condition for the mercy of God to work with you is to *be in God's business*. Brethren, work for God. He is going to pay you more than whatever your earthly boss pays. Luke 2:49, Matthew 28:19 states to "go ye into the world and, make disciples of all nations spread the gospel." This goes to parents as well. The Bible study of today really touches my heart about the present situation of children, not only in America but all over the world. I want to tell you the secret of being a good parent. Early in life, train up your children in the way of the Lord. make your children know Jesus, not as a religion but as a relationship. Make sure your children know the Lord, and the

Lord knows them. Make sure they do what you will expect them to do while away from you. If you want your children to be praying and studying the Bible while in college or anywhere, make sure you are a praying mother and a praise father while they are growing up. Commit them to the hands of God early enough. If you assume that they are children of nowadays, you will encounter the problems of nowadays. That won't be our portion! Do not ignore your children. Don't say this is a civilized world. Commit them to their Creator early in life; He will touch their hearts.

When I was coming to America, I made up my mind to drink a lot of beer because, back home, my parents are pastors, so you dare not. But on getting here, what they had imparted in me, the Bible, prayers, early in life, prevented me from tasting beer up till this present moment. I'm talking to you about all those biblical instructions that come together to guide me to follow Jesus.

It is your responsibility. Don't ignore your children. Don't be tired of standing in the gap for them before the Lord, whether they are with you or not. There's no distance in prayer. And whatever they see you do, they will surely follow suit if you, as a parent, fail in your responsibility to do your background work. There might not be anything your children can learn from you. We have to build them for their God-given destiny because the children God has given unto us are for signs and wonders. Lift your hands toward heaven and call for mercy. It is never too late at any point. Is anybody calling for mercy over your children, academics, career, business, and family? I pray for you today that the mercy of God will work for you in the name of Jesus! The mercy of God will deliver your inheritance to you amongst those that are sanctified in the name of Jesus! Thank You, Lord, for the answered prayers.

I don't like to close this message without inviting Jesus Christ, your Lord and Savior. This may be your first time, or you want to reconnect with Jesus. Pray the prayer after me.

> Lord Jesus, Lord Jesus, Lord Jesus,
> I confess all my sins, and I repent of them.
> I accept you as my Savior.
> I will follow you as my Lord.
> Thank you for saving me. *Amen.*

11/17/2019
THE ATTRIBUTES OF GOD

Brethren, it feels great to stand in the congregation of the people of God today. Do you know that God is the father of our Lord Jesus Christ? Nobody counsels Him. Isaiah 40:13 states, "Who has directed the Spirit of the Lord, or being His counsellor hath taught Him." None encourages Him when He decrees a thing. Every living and nonliving thing is subject to His authority. He is God forever! He changes not. Hallelujah to the Son, the living God! In Jesus's mighty name, we worship. Amen.

If God is glorified, and you are not touched, who else can touch you? Because He is the beginning and the ending of all things. He is God all by Himself. He is the only Being who has no origin. Nobody knows His beginning, and nobody can know His end. Everything in life that has a start date must have an ending date so whatever you are going through now, if it has a start date, must surely have an end date. He created time and brought men to time. He came from eternity to create men and designed time for men that they cannot pass. God cannot be limited to a certain frame of time. He is not thinking about what to do with time because He's above it. God will do what will favor us from now on in Jesus's name. Amen.

Many hear but don't perceive, but God does. Gradually, as we walk with God, He begins to unveil Himself. He is not only a God of crowds. He deals with us individually. In the time of Noah, God called him to construct an ark for Him on a dry surface during the dry season. People began to make fun of Noah because it wasn't even raining yet. But when the rains came, they all ran to him. He couldn't open the door because it was God that shut the door. What I am saying in essence is that whatever door the enemy has shut against you, I see the Lord opening them now in the Name of Jesus!

This God we serve is not human. He is a spirit, so you can always take Him by His words. If there's cordiality between two people, they communicate by their expressions. If you are married to someone, and after a certain time, there's no mutual understanding between you and your spouse, that relationship cannot be described as cordial. This can be likened to our relationship with God. You can know God by His stepping. His words are set to showcase you, bless you, move you to the next level, and advance you. I see God doing all this for us in the name of Jesus!

Knowing who God is, understanding God as our Father is an important aspect in forming our relationship with Him. It forms the basis of acknowledging Him as our Father and also establishes our hope. Whoever steals your hope has stolen your destiny when you are in a hopeless situation. Your destiny is under attack by the devil. But in as much as your hope is alive in God, nobody can steal your destiny. The devil is a liar!

From everlasting to everlasting, God's word is established. His word is sure (Daniel 11:32). Knowing God is a sure foundation for success, when you know Him and He knows you, you shall be strong and do exploits. Anybody can claim to know God, even witches. What matters is whom God recognizes as His own. When God created heaven and earth, He gave dominion to the sons of men. When God possesses a man, He gives His Spirit to him. He descends and speaks through the man to pass His message. The spirit of evil will not take possession of our lives in Jesus' name!

> He made known his ways unto Moses, His acts unto the children of Israel. (Psalm 103:7)

Why was Moses so powerful? Because God chose him as His vessel. He made His heart and His ways known to Moses. When God makes His ways known to you, wonders become your first name. There are many attributes of God that man cannot fully understand unless *He* reveals Himself just like He did to Moses. That is why the people cannot comprehend Him fully.

> Behold, God is great, and we know him not, neither can the number of His years be searched. (Job 36:26)

He reveals Himself to whomever He chooses. Every inventor improves on their inventions. That is why there are different models of inventions to improve on the old models. The only inventor who doesn't need to update His invention is God. His creation is perfect from the beginning through generations. Every invention of God is perfect from inception. He doesn't need to remodel or improve on it. Those that were born in the seventeenth century and eighteenth century have one head, two eyes, two legs, and two hands. and those that were born in the twentieth and centuries to come will still have one head and two eyes. There won't be an improvement that will bring about the third eye at the back of the head. God is perfect the first time. That God is visiting you today, and He will perfect everything that concerns you in the name of Jesus! There can never be an error from God in relation to anything. your case is settled with Him for perfection in the name of Jesus! Amen!

Nobody can know God fully because of our limitedness of a limitless God. Some scientists told us that 75 percent of the human brain has not been put into use. It's still there for generations to tap into. Everything we are looking at today—skyscrapers, bridges, aviation, nuclear and ballistic weapons, fashion, and musical inventions—were all under 25 percent of the human brain utilization. Things that won't allow us to serve God today will become mundane tomorrow. If you travel to Dubai and see the newest models of houses built, this is still part of the 25 percent of the human brain. So when you start to explore the remaining 75 percent, you might start to have an inkling of who God is.

> Great is our Lord and of great power, His understanding is infinite. (Psalm 147:5)

Great is our God.

Who is God? How can you understand Him? God is infinite. He has no origin. He's been alive before life comes to life. He is before all things. Colossians 1:17 states, "By Him all things consist." Everything holds together by the power of God. God opened my mind to Revelation 21:1–3, and I realized there's nothing much to this world. He alone has no end. All other things will come to an end one day. God is everywhere (omnipresent). that will give you the awareness that there's no hiding place before God. You can lie to the pastor or your family members but not to God because He knows the intent of your heart, which is not open to anybody.

God is infinite.

To be infinite is to be without limits. Being truly infinite means God knows no restrictions of space, ability, or power. He is everywhere. There are no edges or limits to His presence nor are there pockets where He is absent. This also means that God is all knowing or that He has unlimited knowledge. His infinite knowledge is what qualifies Him as the sovereign ruler and judge over all things. Not only does God know everything that will happen, but He also knows all things that could have possibly happened. Nothing takes God by surprise, and no one can hide sin from Him.

> For if our heart condemns us, God is greater than
> our heart and knoweth all things. (1 John 3:20)

When you realize that God is infinite, then you will fear *Him* more than your boss. You will not skip church services to please your boss. He is I Am that I Am.

When God sent Moses to Pharaoh, He said to Moses, "Go and tell Pharaoh that I *am* sent you," meaning there's nothing too difficult for Him to do. He can turn the world around in your favor. Your portion of blessings will go with you today in the name of Jesus!

God set boundaries for the seas where they should not pass from the foundation of the earth (Proverbs 8:29). All these things had been set from the beginning. He created two lights—one which is greater to rule the day and the moon for the night. They had never been recharged, no batteries, and they had never failed one minute (Genesis 1:14). It has already been designed for humans to judge their years, age, seasons, time, etc., but God Himself stands outside of time. We cannot control Him because He lives in a timeless zone.

God is immutable.

The immutability of God is an attribute that God is unchanging in His character, will, and covenant promises. God is immutably wise, merciful, good, and gracious (Malachi 3:6).

God is immutable. He never changes. He is the same yesterday, today, and forever (Hebrews 13:8). He is never weary. If you need something from God, take for instance favor, seek and research what someone in a similar situation in the Bible did to compel favor (Acts 10:34) (e.g., Joseph). If you need wisdom, financial breakthrough from God, do what Solomon did, and command the same order of results. Your giving opens the door to prosperity. God can never get stronger or better in your case. He is the same yesterday, today, and forever. He is self-sufficient. He does not need us for anything, but we need Him for everything. And when He is set to do anything, all the angelic hosts swim into action to achieve that which He already set to do.

If God is promising you that, come rain or shine, He will do you favor, rejoice and be glad because victory is already yours despite all odds. He has no needs. He requires help from nobody, but everybody needs help from Him. There's no solution to the challenges of men except God. He is the hope of the hopeless, the help of the helpless, father to the fatherless, mother to the motherless. Be watchful. know the God you are serving. The scripture says, "Those that know their God shall do exploits." You cannot serve God and mammon, said Jesus Christ.

God is self-sufficient.

The true and living God lacks no good thing. He isn't advanced or improved by our existence or efforts. Moreover, God is not dependent upon His creation; rather He is independent of His creation. God does not need us. God did not create the world, the oceans, the lions or the tigers, or the people because He was desperately lonely or lacking. He did not create us to make up for a deficiency in His character attributes. Rather, God is self-existent and self-sufficient. God has no need.

> For as the father hath life in himself, so hath he given the son to have life in himself. (John 5–26)

God is perfectly complete within His own being. The self-sufficiency of God means He possesses infinite riches of being, wisdom, goodness, and power (Genesis 18:14; Jeremiah 32:17; Luke 1:37).

Because God is self-sufficient, we can go to Him to satisfy all our needs.

> Now unto him, that is able to do exceeding abundantly above all that we ask or think, according to the power that worketh in us. (Ephesians 3:20)

Church is meant for sinners, not for only holy people. And when sinners come to Him with a repentant heart ready to follow Him, heaven rejoices. God is perfecting His people unto Jesus to enrapture them for eternity for only those that know and accept Him. In closing today's sermon, let us pray that our lives shall reflect God's glory and His light. Father, prove Yourself in my life. Let the world see me and see Your glory. Amen.

11/24/2019
THE POTENCY OF THANKSGIVING

> Enter His gates with thanksgiving and His court with praise, be thankful unto Him and bless His name. (Psalm 100–4)

> Do not be anxious about anything, but in every situation, by prayer and petition, with thanksgiving, present your requests to God. (Philippians 4–6)

God is a pathfinder, waymaker. Faithful Jesus! That God will show you mercy in the mighty name of Jesus!

When He shows up, He shows off. He has all the power. Absolute power is in His hands. He created all things, He created things that cannot be imagined. He is before existence. He has been before the beginning. He is now and forever. He will be when there's nothing on the surface of the earth. He is the judge of all. He has been before creation, and He will always be. For your case to be impossible, He will change government for your glory to not shine. God will remove somebody, replace somebody, disconnect somebody in the name of Jesus. How can you be sons and daughters of God and someone will be harassing you when authority in heaven and on earth has been placed on your shoulder? Jesus died for your cause. He died for you so you can live for *Him*. He gave us a key. Jesus said He has given you the keys of the house of David and that whatever you decree in this world shall be established in heaven. Whatever you cancel or establish on earth shall be so in heaven. Anybody that says your glory will not shine, the Lord will remove them in the name of Jesus!

I'm talking to you today about the potency of thanksgiving. When you give thanks, what happens? When you give thanks to God, what changes you are expected to see? It is not happy people that are thankful, it is thankful people that are happy. Thanksgiving is an attitude of gratitude that enhances your attitude in life, meaning that if you want to go up, all you need do is to send your praise up because when your praise goes up, what comes down is blessings. It is the degree of your gratitude that defines your rating in the kingdom of God. The more you can complain, the more you remain. But the more you can praise, the more you are raised. People that are raised in the Bible are notable for giving praises to God. That is why, He kept elevating them because when you praise God, you are bound to receive blessings from His hands. Why is it when you pray, you are asking God to do something, but when you praise, you are celebrating His mightiness? He comes down and inhabits the praises (Psalm 22:3). He doesn't allow your praise to come down to you when you praise Him because when you pray, your prayer ascends to heaven, according to Revelation 8:3, and stay at the right side of the saints to be answered. But when you praise, God comes down to accept your praise and to give you blessings in return. Therefore, if God is for you, who can be against you? Nobody on earth can be against you.

Thanksgiving is being grateful for all the blessings of God when you look at everything around you and you are able to give thanks to God.

> Bless the Lord, O my soul, and forget not all His benefits. (Psalm 103:2)

Many of us, because of our education, connections, and ego, think where we are is too low to our standard that it is not a good place for us. Why am I here struggling? Why am I at this level? But we have failed to realize that many of our agemates are six feet below the ground. Many of us complain a lot, forgetting those of our mates in psychiatric homes who don't recognize the essence of time, no more but some people kept complaining about having not enough food, no pretty money, etc. A brother fell sick some time ago. He was taken to the hospital and from there to the rehabilitation center. Altogether he spent two years. For those two years, he was unconscious. Thank God he came around to consciousness. The day he came to church to give testimony, he said that for those two years, it was as if he just slept and woke up overnight. For those two years, he was oblivious to the happenings around him. He was not aware at all for two years.

When you acknowledge what God has done for you, when you are not only looking at one dark side alone, but you are able to look at the other bright side, not being selfish. What of the people in the mortuary or nursing homes who died rich but could no longer spend their money? But God already decorated your life. You are well seated, and you have hope that things are going to be better by the day. Psalm 103:2 states, "Bless the Lord, oh my soul, and forget not all His benefits." There are some benefits that the world or money cannot give, like the free air we breathe. Thanksgiving is to recognize that it is not our attitude or aptitude that changes our altitude, it is God's mercy all the way.

> I will extol thee, O Lord, for thou has lifted me
> up and has not made my foes to rejoice over me.
> (Psalm 30:1)

> But the meek shall inherit the earth, and shall
> delight themselves in the abundance of peace.
> (Psalm 37:11)

One of the sisters in the church during her birthday thanksgiving posted on her wall that she thanked God for the free oxygen she breathes since the day she was born. That's a big one! Nobody here can afford the cost of oxygen. Nobody! To have a heart transplant alone, which is subject to availability even if you have the money, might not be available or compatible. But those are the organs that function in you. And when you look at yourself, you can jump, reason, see, breathe at will, dance, walk around. Why can't we praise God? Alleluia to the Son of God!

The easy way to victory is thanksgiving. It is not the intensity of your prayer but the gravity of your praise that calls the attention of heaven. When you want to secure the attention of God, please turn to thanksgiving. Engage in praiseworthy songs. When you want God to turn to your side, engage Him in thanksgiving because the Bible says He dwells in the praise of His people (Psalm 22:3). So when your praises go up, God comes down to challenge all your challengers and silence all those who want to oppress your life. I see the Lord silencing all those that want to oppress you in the name of Jesus!

Acts 16:25 states that Paul and Silas were chained because they preached the gospel and cast out demons from the person afflicted with evil spirits. As they began to engage in praise, the prisoners heard them. Their praise ascended to heaven, and God came down to loosen their chains. When you praise, and God is coming for you, He even blesses those around you after blessing you because not only Paul's and Silas's chains were loosened but also all the other prisoners around them, and they were set free. I see the Lord stepping out for your glory today in the name of Jesus. Amen!

When you keep praising God, then better days are still ahead. When you stop praising God, blessings stop. When you are tired of praising God, then you are retired. When a man stops thanking God, his tank becomes empty. But when a man is thankful, his tank is full. When you run out of food in the house, all you need do is to be thankful because God will ordain your feet to where goodness and mercy will follow you. You know what Jesus did when they ran out of food in the crusade ground and was left with five loaves of bread and two pieces of fishes? He gave thanksgiving, and the canteen in heaven resumed production of bread and fishes so much so that excess twelve baskets were left behind (John 6:1–14). Am I talking to somebody? When you are faced with a difficult situation, the Lord will step down to make you victorious over it.

When you thank God for what you have not received from Him, He is compelled to bring it into existence and to give you more. I want you to stand up for two minutes and give Him praise. Give Him praise. Alleluia!

Thanksgivers never beg because the power of multiplication is in their tongues. Remember the boy with two little fishes and five loaves in John 6? Jesus never begged. He raised the loaves and the fishes to heaven, and the Bible recorded that He gave *thanks*. After Jesus gave thanks, immediately the canteen of heaven was opened. All the caterers in heaven swung into action to produce fishes and bread and began sending them into the world. All the workers in heaven worked overtime that day to answer to the request of our Lord Jesus Christ, and the food was supplied, and they had excess. I see heaven working overtime for your sake in the name of Jesus! No matter how much money you have, either in the bank or your wallet or your home, today will mark your minimum. You will go from glory to glory, from victory to victory, from honor to honor in the name of Jesus!

When you are a thanksgiver, you only walk through the valley of the shadows of death. King David said in Psalm 23:4, "Though I walk *through* the valley of the shadow of death". He only walked *through*; he was unscathed. It might affect others. Others might get punished or afflicted. But it won't affect you. All you are doing is walking through. You only walk through. You are not hurt in any way. You are not affected. It doesn't stop you. Can you tell somebody close to you, "I'm walking through to my success, honor, walking through to a better day. Keep on walking through. The Lord is on your side. You are coming out victorious."

I love the USA for being a country that gives thanks. In all circumstances, they set aside a day to give thanks to God.

What are you thanking God for? Every time you take money to the bank, do you think it's by your power or ability? No. Unless the Lord builds the house, they labor in vain that build it. It is the Lord that sustains you. It is the Lord that is your keeper and your helper. Somebody, shout Alleluia to the Son of God!

How best to present your thanksgiving

The four ways that you can quickly present your thanksgiving:

1. *The prayer of thanksgiving.* You can offer thanksgiving to God by prayer, thanking God for your life, for where you are coming from, for the glorious destination He is taking you; don't forget it—prayer of thanksgiving. Don't just wake up in the morning and start murmuring, No! Give thanks to God, for He is good, and His mercies endure forever. Give thanks to God for sparing your life and that of your children. Wake up in the morning with a positive attitude and thank God. Open your mouth on bent knees and offer your prayer of thanks. Philippians 4:6 states, "Be careful for nothing." What are you careful for—job, marriage, money? But look, the scriptures say to be careful for nothing! But in everything with prayer and thanksgiving, let your request be made known to God.

    When you give thanks to God, saying, Father, I thank you today. I'm just living in a room in the house, but I'm believing you for better accommodation. God is going to come down and do it. If you thank God for being alive though you don't have plenty of money in the bank, God is going to come down and satisfy your body, soul, and spirit with good things.

For He satisfies the thirsty and fills the hungry
with good things. (Psalm 107:9)

   When a man with both legs was complaining, God showed him someone who has no legs at all. Be careful, for nothing is the counsel of the children of God. When you stay in one room and give thanks for your situation, God can give you a better place beyond your wildest dream.

   God does not want to be part of your life; He wants to be first. If he is not first, then He is not there. He has to be first in your schedule. He has to be first in your spending and in everything you do. When you wake up in the morn-

ing, the first twenty minutes should be dedicated to God, not Facebook or cell phone.
2. *Worship and praise thanksgiving.* You can sing praises and worship God. You can praise Him to thank Him for all He has done. When you wake up in the morning, on your way to the bathroom or work, you can engage in songs of thanksgiving. God is cleaning the day and going ahead of you to perfect it; but when you wake up in the morning and say there's no food, no money, nothing is working, God is not happy. forget about the issues of yesterday. Wake up with thanksgiving. Go into your living room with songs of thanksgiving. Let someone in your household ask what is making you so happy even if you don't have your house rent yet. Tell them the great provider will provide. Don't import the issues of yesterday into today's affair (Psalm 100:4).
3. *The testimony of thanksgiving.* This is when you share your testimony with others, when you tell others about what the Lord has done for you: "I was once blind, but now I can see." "I was sick, but the Lord healed me." "I needed a helper. The Lord raised it up for me." "I was once in a difficult situation, but God has elevated me." When you share your testimony, you receive more, and God will keep working for you. Don't be afraid to share your testimonies amongst your coworkers everywhere you go to everyone you come across with. Revelation 12:11 says, "They overcame him by the blood of the Lamb and the words of their testimonies, and they loved not their lives unto death."
4. *The offering of thanksgiving.*
Leviticus 7:13–15. You might decide to bring anything to the house of God. Any offerings at all, both monetary and material, are referred to as offerings of thanksgiving. You have to be resolute, not under duress. Nobody must force you to do it. Anything you do under compulsion is not acceptable to God. It has to be from your heart packaged from your house. God will accept that kind of thanksgiving and bless you.

12/01/2019
THE OIL OF GLADNESS AND FAVOR

> Thou lovest righteousness, and hated wickedness; therefore God, thy God hath anointed thee with the oil of gladness above thy fellows. All thy garments smell of myrrh and aloes and cassia, out of the ivory palaces whereby they have made thee glad. (Psalm 45, 7–8)

> Thou shall arise and have mercy upon zion; for the time to favour her, yea the set time, is come. For thy servant take pleasure in her stone and favour the dust thereof. So the heathen shall fear the name of the Lord and all the kings of the earth thy glory. (Psalm 102:13–15)

Is there anyone in the house that can claim the proclamation of prayer that can say amen to prayers? Amen means "so let it be." When a prayer is said, and you say amen, you are saying, "God, let it be so unto me." You shall never encounter sorrow in the mighty name of Jesus!

I will be talking to you in what is called the oil of gladness and favor, which is so rare. It is not common. It comes out occasionally. It only surfaces when God calls it out. That is the kind of oil the Lord is bringing to you today. It is the oil that will give you your inheritance among those that are sanctified (Acts 20:32), the oil that will settle your life (Genesis 45:10), the oil that will promote you (Psalm 75:6–7), the oil that will take you far above your capacity and your connection (Psalm 121:1). The oil will settle you financially, health wise, and in every angle that you turn (3 John 1:2). It is the oil of the blessed. It is the oil that anoints kings. The oil will turn you into a noble. It will make you kings and queens. that is what the oil will do for us in the mighty name of Jesus!

God is so good to us in every circumstance and condition. Take a good look at yourself and see where God is bringing you from to where you are today and where He is taking you in the future. Look at the promises of God to you. He said that eyes have not seen, ears have not heard. It has never come to mind the good things that the Lord has in store for you. God has beautiful things beyond the human mind, beyond human comprehension. The Lord has all these in store for you. You might be in need of one thing today, but what God has in store for you is way more than what you can imagine. You might be thinking, *Where is the way?* But God is a waymaker. He can make a way out of nowhere. God will make a way where there is no way. He does not need to struggle before making a way. He doesn't have to lament before making a way because He is a pathfinder and a waymaker.

The special oil of gladness and favor will qualify you for four things: *hand, face, voice, message.* Everything good you begin to see now, God will begin to give it to you from heaven as a gift. God will suspend your labor and give you favor. Your effort will be small, but the result will be great in the name of Jesus! You don't have to work like an elephant and eat like an ant no more. The time has come, which is a time of harvest, the time that God is going to decorate your life, the time the Lord will help you out for that thing that seems impossible to you. The Lord Himself will do it for you.

Anointing of today is the anointing of favor. Favor is the mother of destiny. Your life can never be colorful more than the extent of favor accessible to you. The more you are favored, the more of God you enjoy. Many people struggling in the world had never enjoyed the favor of God. When you experience the favor of heaven, you sweat less because heaven is working on your behalf. The goodness and mercy of God are following you. The protection of heaven is upon your life. When you decree a thing, it is established in heaven. When you sneeze, your enemy catches a cold. When the favor of God is upon your life, you ask in the morning and receive immediately. You ask in the afternoon; you receive in the afternoon. You ask in the evening; you receive in the evening. You ask in the night; you receive in the night Isaiah 65:24. That is your portion in the name of Jesus!

I bind every spirit of lukewarmness in the name of Jesus! Alleluia to the Son of God! When God accepts or has selected you, it does not matter who else has rejected or neglected you because God's favor outweighs all opposition. If God is for you, there's no enemy in view. When God establishes our steps into a case, nobody can cancel it. If God cancels a case before you, nobody can reopen it. He has the final authority on everything living or dead.

He is the ancient of days. He has all the wisdom and ability. He does whatever pleases Him. He is the ancient of days. All wisdom belongs to him. He doesn't consult anybody before taking any decision. He doesn't take advice from anyone. All the powers in heaven and on earth are in the hands of God. Nobody advises Him. He has absolute authority over all the issues of life. I see that God is at work on your behalf in the name of Jesus!

Although some people might have not achieved all their expectations up till now, I want you to look at something in Habakkuk 3:17–19.

> Although the fig tree shall not blossom, neither shall fruit be in the vines; the labour of the olive shall fail, and the fields shall yield no meat; the flock shall be cut off from the fold and there shall be no herd in the stalls, yet I will rejoice in the Lord, I will joy in the God of my salvation. The lord God is my strength, and he will make my feet like hinds' feet and he will make me to walk upon mine high places to the chief singer on my stringed instrument.

It says, "Although the fig tree might not blossom." Listen to this because many people will say, up till now, they have not gotten what they are asking from God. He is saying to you today to *wait*! There might be things you are still expecting God to do for you but haven't gotten it yet, but He says to you today to rejoice because God's timing is different from yours. He is saying to you that He is the one that lives outside time, so His timing and yours differ. He is asking you to wait for His timing. When His time comes, the glory of the latter house shall be greater than the former. The glory that God is going to give you tomorrow is better than that of yesterday.

Let me tell you, if you buy a car in 2002, and then you buy another one in 2020, which one will be newer, better, and preferred? Am I talking to somebody! If you build a house in 2000, and you build another one in 2020, which one will be more beautiful? Definitely, what God is planning in your life by the time He finishes packaging and delivering it to you, the world will envy you. When you haven't received what you are looking for, there's a solution (Hebrews 12:2). Now see what the Bible says: If you are looking for something but haven't gotten it, the Bible says, "Looking unto Jesus the author and finisher of our faith who for the joy that was set before Him endured the cross." You see, the reason Jesus endured the cross is that there's a particular glory ahead of Him.

Joy is more of focus than of feeling. Many of us are where we are today for one reason. Many of us live comfortable lives, but we are looking and still working to better the lots of our children. That is why we are working smart and hard. Somebody said to me, "Pastor, I spent all my earnings on my children. I have just a little saving." I told him it is an investment that is worth doing. You might not have money today. So far, you are not gambling with it. You are investing it in your children or training yourself in school or other business. All these are investments that are worth doing. Don't complain. Don't murmur because there's a joy that God has set for you. You will receive it and achieve all your aim in the name of Jesus.

The anointing oil will guarantee four things. when you receive it you will see the following:

1. *The hand of favor.* That is the number one thing that I want you to watch out for: the hand of favor. Do you know what the hand of favor will do for you? (1 Kings 18:46). After Elijah told Ahab that it was going to rain in the land, he told Ahab to go back to his palace in the city because there had been famine in the land of Samaria due to the lack of rain for three and half years. So on the day it was about to rain, the prophet of the Most High God spoke to the king to start heading back to the city because they were on the mountain. The prophet told him the rain would fall before he gets to his palace, so immediately the king mounted his chariot to race back to his palace. The Bible says that the hand of the favor of God rested upon Elijah, and he outran the chariot and got to the city. Let me tell you what the hand of favor will do for you: What has been difficult for you to achieve for the past ten years, in a matter of ten minutes, the Lord will give it to you in the name of Jesus! The hand of favor will make you actualize what you had been struggling for despite all your mates that had gone ahead of you. All those people that you believe had left you behind, that made you feel you no longer matter to them, who believe they had gone far from you—today, when this anointing touches your head, the Lord will bring the hand of favor upon you, and you will outshine them in the name of Jesus. Amen!

   When the hands of favor rest upon you, it gives you what you cannot achieve by your labor in ten years. When Isaac was in Philistines, there was a famine in the land. This man had no father. Abraham, his father had died. He is the only man in a strange land, and everyone was making jest of him because he had no father, no food, no house. He was sleeping on a cliff. His condition was pitiable. They asked him, "Where is the God you claimed serving?" Isaac was struggling; and because of that, he wanted to run away. But when he was planning to run away, the spirit of the Lord and the hand of favor rested upon him and told him, "Isaac, don't run in this famine season. Now begin to sow seed." And Isaac went out and began to sow seed. There was no rain for three years—no dew, no moisture. But because of the word of God and the hands of favor of God upon Isaac, he began to sow. Then all the Philistines came around and made jest of him. "Isaac, are you insane? You are sowing seed on dry ground." But he did not listen to them. He began to do what the Lord commanded him. The Bible says, in the same year, he yielded a hundred percent return. He had an abundance of food. He had an abundance of everything. Do you know what later happened? Those Philistines that were earlier making jest of him came back to beg him, "Isaac, let us be your servants. You be our master." Let me tell you what, everything you have been struggling to achieve, when the anointing touches you, you will outshine your mates in the name of Jesus!

In the end, the Philistines began to ask him to hire and feed them. "Isaac let us make you our king because you are the only one who can feed us." I pray for you today, if you can say amen that the king of glory will raise you up, and you will begin to feed your enemy in the name of Jesus. You might be thinking you haven't achieved anything, but when God raises you up and you begin to feed your enemy when your enemy starts asking you for money and help and you are able to feed them, that is the hand of God's favor. Your enemy will not die, but he will see your glory. Amen! The hand of favor, when it rests upon you, will elevate you. It paves the way for you miraculously beyond man's efforts. Everybody will know that this is the hand of God.

The young man that came to our church, looking for papers to live here, went to the immigration office. The man he met said he wasn't going to attend to him, but his supervisor would. By the spirit of God, I told him to go meet the supervisor. The hand of the favor of God rested upon this man, and the supervisor tore all the wrong documentation in his file and reinstated him as a green card holder. What his effort could not achieve, under ten minutes, the hand of favor got it for him. I stand upon this altar, and I declare what you have been struggling for and cannot achieve. The hand of the favor of God will release it upon your life in the name of Jesus!

2. *Face of favor.* This anointing of today will give you a face of favor. In Numbers 6:25, it states, "The Lord make His face shine upon thee, and be gracious to thee."

The Lord commanded the priest and said, "This is how you should bless my people." The Lord makes His face shine upon you and be gracious to you. This anointing oil will guarantee you the face of God. When the face of God shines upon you, it is called glory. The face of God will shine upon your health matters, circumstances, marital issues, finances, upon anything that challenges you in the name of Jesus!

When the face of God shines upon you, all the angels of God are keeping you in their focus, and then they speed up everything that will make you joyful. He says that the Lord makes His face shine upon you so you are receiving the face of favor. God will make His face shine upon you, and nobody will be able to say no to you when you knock on any door. The spirit of God sent a message to a man that I knew. The spirit of God told him that he had no house of his own, no savings, and he had been working for his state government for long. So God promised to build a house for him. But the man responded that he is an upright man who cannot steal any dime from the government. God said, "I, the Lord, will build a house for you. I will cause my face to shine on you then you will build a house. When the covenant was made, we were all rejoicing. Listen to me; two months after this proclamation was made, they lied against him in the ministry where he worked, and he was fired. The news was everywhere after two months of God's prophecy. Ordinarily, we might be thinking, some powers were working against his prophecy, probably, in the church or outside. But no! Nobody knows the way of the Lord. He came back to church, but God told him that He didn't see his termination letter. Instead, God told him He saw his promotion letter. How was this going to be? No one knew, only God. For one and half years, he went on without a job. He went to the church office every day to help out, and the spirit of God kept telling him, "You are working. No one will fire you." A day came when they reviewed the case, and the government realized that they lied against him because the men involved in the case confessed. He was never part of the fraud. The governor had to apologize to this man, and all the salaries of the past years were paid in full. He also got promoted. This money was what this man used to buy land and build his house where he lives till date, and all the prophecies were fulfilled according to the word of the Lord.

God will do something that will embarrass your enemy. God will do something that will make the enemy realize you are serving a living God. the face of God will shine on you in the mighty name of Jesus!

3. *The voice of favor.* Second Samuel 9:1 states, "And David said, is there yet any that is left of the house of Saul, that I may shew him kindness for Jonathan's sake?" King David rose up and called his servant Seba and said, Is there yet someone left in the house of Saul that I can show him favor for Jonathan's sake? Seba said that there was a boy left whose name was Mephibosheth. He was living a wretched life in the village where he went hungry all day. So King David ordered the boy to be brought before him. The king told him, "All the land and properties your father worked for, all the money the government had taken from your father, I'm returning it to you." The king said Seba's fifteen sons and twelve daughters would be working for Mephibosheth.

One day, the voice of favor came to this boy, and his life changed forever. This was a crippled who had no idea where his next meal would come from. When the voice of favor came to him, David called Seba and told him to return his field of gold back to Mephibosheth. The field of gold, the one that belonged to your fathers, is restored to you today in the name of Jesus! The glory that belongs to your father's lineage is returned to you in the name of Jesus. The voice and the favor of God are coming to you. The Lord will supply you with what the world cannot take away from you in the name of Jesus.

If God can take somebody from the gutter and put them with princes and princesses, He will do more for you. The Lord will change your story to glory.

4. *The message of favor.*

And the angel came in unto her and said, Hail, thou that art highly favoured, the Lord is with thee; blessed art thou among women. (Luke 1:28)

And Mary said, Behold the handmaid of the Lord; be it unto me according to thy word. And the angel departed from her. (Luke 1:33)

When you receive this message of favor, it changes your life. Look at it. A decision was made in heaven. And without the beneficiary being brought into the picture, Angel Gabriel was sent to deliver a message to Mary because she is highly favored. Mary was going to conceive and deliver a child and call him Jesus who was going to deliver the world from sin—that is called a message of favor. Some messages will just come from the throne of grace to favor you.

For those of us looking up to heaven, good news from the throne of grace will come to our ears in the name of Jesus. Despite many who may doubt the authority of heaven, I cancel your doubt, and your glory will shine because it has been established in heaven.

Before the end of this year, a decision will be made in heaven that will impact your life positively forever. God's message of favor will arrive at your destination in the name of Jesus. It's called the message of favor. It will just come in a way that you cannot comprehend.

Favor is not fair. When God wants to favor you, He surpasses your enemies. He suppresses your antagonists. God can demote some people to elevate you. When God wants to surprise you, He changes power.

For all these favors, the hand, face, voice, and message of favor to happen in your life, there are requirements. I say it time and time again, the only thing that is free in this kingdom is salvation because Jesus paid for it. He paid with His own blood. Every other thing that you want to receive in the kingdom of God, you have to have a hand in it. You have a part to play. There is one requirement for all these favors to work in your life. Hebrews 1:9 states, "Thou hast loved righteousness and hated iniquity." For God to anoint you with the oil of gladness above your contemporaries, you must love righteousness and hate sin. That is just the requirement. It is easy.

When you run away from sin and show obedience—total obedience—do what God wants you to do. It's as simple as ABC. That is just the requirement.

Tithe is part of obedience. It is a demand (Matthew 23:23). That is what opens the windows of heaven for your blessings to come down.

Time—your time—how many times were you present in the house of God or involved in the activities of the house of God. God values your effort and time more than money. How much time do you spend checking on other church members? How much time do you spend on evangelism, on visitation? When you comply with this standard, God values it, and you are open to receiving oil of gladness and favor. When you are sick, the first covenant of contact is the blood of Jesus (Isaiah 53:5). Don't think of your doctor first. Think about the blood of Jesus before your doctor. Proclaim that you are healed by His stripes, that you are covered by the precious blood of Jesus. Think about that first, however, when you pray and meet with your doctor. God will assist your doctor to help you out.

When you need a financial breakthrough, tithing is a covenant requirement. When you need healing, the covenant is the blood of Jesus. When you need the fruit of the womb, your service to the Lord is required (Exodus 23:25). When you want God to open doors for you, it is your service to the Lord. Attend church services on time. Sing praises, and then God will send His angels to open your path of favor. Let's rise up for prayers. Pray this prayer: Father Lord, I want the oil of gladness to come upon my life. I want the hand, face, voice, and message of favor to work wonders in my life. Is someone praying? This prayer will usher into your life the anointing oil of favor in the name of Jesus Christ! Amen.

I don't want to end this message without giving you the opportunity to make Jesus your Lord and Savior. Please pray this prayer after me:

> Lord Jesus, Lord Jesus, Lord Jesus,
> I confess my sin and repent of it.
> I accept you as my Savior.
> I will follow you as my Lord
> Thank you for saving me. Amen.

12/08/20
DIVINE LIBERTY

> Stand fast therefore in the liberty wherewith Christ hath made us free and not entangled again with the yoke of bondage. (Galatians 5:1)
>
> Now the lord is that Spirit; and where the spirit of the Lord is, there is liberty. (2 Corinthians 3:17)
>
> If the son therefore shall make you free, ye shall be free indeed. (John 8:36)

The greatest gift God has given man is freedom, liberty (Psalm 119:45). You are not under any pressure. Nothing is holding you down. God gives you freedom. The sermon and words of the Holy Spirit we hear on daily basis are teaching us the benefits of Christianity, what you gain from being a Christian. Do you know that when you know everything God has given to you, when you understand the benefits you get from Christ, when you understand the true meaning of what Jesus has done, when you understand what you stand to gain as a Christian, there's no way you can live like a slave? It is very important for Christians to understand this. That's why the scriptures say, "My people perish for lack of knowledge" (Hosea 4:6).

For example, a child who doesn't know his father is the richest man in the world will still go out and beg for food because he doesn't know. But the moment he understands how wealthy his father is, it becomes very difficult for him to beg. As Christians, it is important to understand these things that God has freely given unto us.

Today, we are looking into what we call divine liberty. You can also say divine freedom, absolute liberty, complete immunity. You are completely free. During the course of this sermon, we will be looking into the kind of freedom God gave us: freedom from fear, anxiety, curses, sin, and death. It is important to hold your Bible because we will be looking into the Bible extensively. This sermon will open our eyes to those free things that God has given unto us already. What makes the life of a Christian meaningful is when you understand what Jesus has done for you. But when you don't, then any fake pastor can easily mislead you to do what is wrong, and you begin to run with it.

Let's open our Bible to 1 Corinthians 2:12.

> Now we have received not the Spirit of the world, but the Spirit which is of God; that we might know the things that are freely given to us of God.

It says we have received the Spirit of God that will make us understand those things that God has freely given unto us. This is the reason, in John 16:7, Jesus told His disciples that it is a must for me to go that He has a lot of things to tell them, but they couldn't bear it. But when he leaves, then the spirit of truth, which His Father will send in His name, will reveal all things to them.

> Nevertheless I tell you the truth; it is expedient for you that I go away; for if I go not away, the comforted will not come unto you; but if I depart I will send him unto you. (John 16:7)

Without the Holy Spirit, it becomes extremely difficult for us to know the benefits of what Jesus has done. And that is why, in Christianity, nobody can undermine the importance of the Holy Spirit. It is not just what we can do without. No! There's a place for

God the Father, Son, and the Holy Spirit. You cannot say God is bigger than the Holy Spirit. It is the same God manifesting Himself in different dispensations. The dispensation we are right now is that of the Holy Spirit. That is why Jesus said that when the Holy Spirit comes, He will guide His disciples into all truth.

The Spirit of God gives you the capacity and ability to receive the total package of God, which He brings. He carries God as a whole and brings God into you. That's how the Spirit of God functions. That's why I want us to take note of that thing which God has freely given unto us. If you don't know it, a Christian can leave like a servant for the rest of his life. Jesus told His disciples to stay in Jerusalem. There's a reason He said that to them. He did not say, "Until you begin to speak in tongues." No, it is more than that. A lot of us, when they talk about Pentecost, our minds go straight to speaking in tongues; but it is more than that. What was the power Jesus told His disciples to stay and wait to receive in Jerusalem? It was the power and ability to fulfill what God had called them to do. So the Spirit of God is very important. First John 3:8 says, "He that committeth sin is of the devil; for the devil sinneth from the beginning. For this purpose, the son of God was manifested that he might destroy the works of the devil."

He that commits sin is of the devil because he sinned from the beginning. The works of the devil in this context are to put people in bondage to blindfold people so that they don't know what they can do. He creates fear and anxiety in people the moment you are fearful or anxious, then you won't be able to maximize your potentials. All the devil did in the Old Testament was to put people in captivity. He blindfolded their minds. They couldn't see beyond where they were, so they saw God as a threat, an angry God. No wonder when Moses came back from the mount, all the Israelites could do was to cover their faces (Exodus 34: 29–35). They could not see God the way He was because the devil did not want them to see Him as that loving and merciful Father. So he put them in that bondage, and that is why the Bible says that the Son of Man was manifested to destroy the works of Satan.

Apostle Paul was so clear when he said that Jesus came to break down the barrier between us and God just to give us freedom (Ephesians 2:14), "which is the earnest of our inheritance until the redemption of the purchased possession, unto the praise of his glory." These things we have to understand to be able to claim our liberty in Christ Jesus. I pray that God will help us in Jesus's name!

> For brethren, ye have been called unto liberty;
> only use not liberty for an occasion to the flesh,
> but by love serve one another. (Galatians 5:13)

1. *Called unto liberty.* Everything Jesus came to do was just to give us the liberty to free our minds. He understood that the best way to enslave a man is to fill his mind with anxiety. For example, a man who is depressed is a walking dead. They take them off the streets, so the devil knows that all you need to enslave a man is to clog his mind. The moment you do that, you have taken all the potentials of that man away. The same thing with every one of us. When we sit in our houses, and all we can think about is our problems, challenges, the fact remains from that moment on. Every ability you have had been sidelined because of the blindfold of the devil. That is why Jesus came to free us from the bondage of the devil.
2. *Freedom from fear.* This can also be termed "absence of faith." Where there is fear, doubt abounds, weakness thrives, and it is difficult for God to operate in an environment of fear. Fear does not allow people to move forward. When you allow fear and negativity, it slows a man down. When God is operating, He does not want anything to slow Him down because He is a God of time and purpose. John 14:27 states, "Peace I leave with you, my peace I give unto you; not as the world giveth, give I unto you. Let not your heart be troubled, neither let it be afraid."

   It says not to let our hearts be troubled. The moment you are troubled, as a Christian, you worry a lot. It becomes a celebration to the devil. Second Timothy 1:7 says that He has not given us the spirit of fear but that of power, love, and a sound mind. Anything that has to do with fear is not of God. Take a look at anybody who is sick. The moment they become fearful, what happens is that death comes knocking. That is why it is important for us to be strong-minded in the Lord and proclaim life, instead of death.

For ye have not receive the spirit of bondage again to fear; but ye have received the spirit of adoption, whereby we cry Abba Father. (Romans 8:15)

    It says that we have not received the spirit of bondage. Everything that has to do with bondage has been removed but replaced with the spirit of adoption. Do we know why Apostle Paul used the word "adoption"? Because we are joint heirs of the father (Romans 8:17) because I'm a part of God's family. That is why we are entitled to everything in Christ. This is the mentality that God wants us to live with. Once we confess these things in our hearts, it registers. And when the spirit man receives it, your life begins to operate in that fashion.

3. *Freedom from sin and death.* This is the most important point today. Jesus came to set us free from sin and death. Let's go to Galatians 5:1: "Stand firm in that liberty." Do everything possible to walk in liberty. Jesus had done what He came to do so that we don't fall back to sin. What are those things that can entangle a Christian? The common thing that we all know is sin. So the earlier we stay away from sin, the better. The Bible commands us to flee from every appearance of evil after we have been saved (1 Thessalonians 5–22). Don't throw your liberty to the dogs.

Likewise reckon ye also yourselves to be dead indeed unto sin, but alive unto God through

Jesus Christ our lord. Let not sin therefore reign in your mortal body, that ye should obey it in the lust thereof. Neither yield ye your members as instruments of unrighteousness unto sin but yield yourselves unto God, as those that are alive from the dead and your members as instruments of righteousness unto God for sin shall not have dominion over you; for ye are not under the law, but under grace. (Romans 6:11–14)

Whomever you yield yourself to becomes your master. If you walk in the path of sin, it becomes your master. If you walk in the way of righteousness, it becomes your way of life. These things need to be in our minds as Christians. The Spirit of God that we have been talking about hates sin, so the earlier we yield ourselves to God, the better (Habakkuk 1:13).

4. *Freedom from ignorance.* The Bible made it clear in John 8:32 that "Ye shall know the truth and, the truth shall set you free." The truth is Jesus (John 14:6). When you open yourself to the truth, you become free. When you open yourself to Christ—the ideas that will flow to you, the intuition, the inspiration you get, what comes to your mind—you will know that you are free. It will even reflect in your daily affairs.

Ignorance has the highest death rate in the world. If you say wisdom is expensive, try ignorance. But God has given us freedom from ignorance, so it is left to us to walk into knowledge. Deuteronomy 8:18 says to remember the Lord your God who has given you the power to make wealth. That power to make wealth, if you break it down, means knowledge, ability, direction, favor—everything you need to make wealth.

The main cause of ignorance is arrogance. Others are negative beliefs that become indisputable facts (like some-

one fighting for God on the ground of religion), willingness to give up the power of thinking, believing everything you have been told without verifying, and choosing denial rather than facing the implication of what is obvious.
5. *Freedom from curse.*

Christ hath redeemed us from the curse of the law being made a curse for us; for it is written, cursed is everyone that hangeth on a tree. (Galatians 3:13)

A lot has been duped at one time or the other in the past because of that general word—generational curse—which God has already redeemed us from by His precious blood (Deuteronomy 21:23). This is where God placed a curse on anyone hanged on the tree. Let us go to Galatians 3:13. This is Apostle Paul making references to where we read earlier. This is why Jesus was hanged on the tree so that he could free us from every curse from Adam to the last person on earth. Jesus had taken them away, meaning that I'm free. Colossians 2:14–15 gives us more explanation: "Blotting out the handwriting of ordinances." Jesus took out all our challenges from our way and nailed them to the cross. He made an open show of shame of our enemies.

6. *Freedom from anxiety.* A lot of people suffer from anxiety. It's a killer of destiny. First Peter 5:7 states, "Casting all your care upon him for he careth for you."

Cast all your cares, all your worries, everything bothering your mind. God has given us an open check. You don't have to sit down and worry so much. All you need to do is to take all these issues and hand them over to God because He cares for you. All God wants for us is our well-being. He is not happy when we worry about things we have no control over. The only thing we should worry about is when we have the ability to do something, but we refuse to do it probably due to spiritual laziness or physical that's not God's issue. It's ours to deal with, but issues that are beyond us are meant to be pushed over to God and pray. Philippians 4:6 says "Be anxious for nothing." Don't worry unnecessarily. Why are we worried? Just play your part and leave the rest for God. A lot of people gathered around Jesus, but that woman with the issue of blood understood that she should touch the hem of His garment. So she tried moving close to Him, and the result she got was fantastic. All we need to do is play our part and move close to God.

12/15/2019
THE POWER OF THE ATTITUDE

Do all things without murmurings and disputings. (Philippians 2:14)

Finally, brethren, whatsoever things are true, whatsoever things are honest, whatsoever things are just, whatsoever things are lovely, whatsoever things are of good report, if there be any virtue and if there be any praise, think on these things. (Philippians 4:8–9)

God has packaged it in the heavenlies and released it upon our lives that in the world we are going into, we will not be tail; rather we will be the head (Deuteronomy 28:13). He has packaged it for us that salvation, joy, protection are our portion. Such joy will rest upon our lives in the name of Jesus! We thank God Almighty because He is faithful. He is God forever. Absolute power belongs to Him. He is the only one that makes a promise and fulfills it, for it is not in anyone to fulfill promises except God. He doesn't consult your past to determine your future. When He stops, the whole world bows down to succumb. Authority answers Him in heaven. When He sneezes, thunder blows from heaven. He is a majestic, awesome, all sufficient, ever reliable, ever dependable, trustworthy God, ancient of days, the wonderful counselor, the great King. That God will be sufficient for you in the name of Jesus!

For the remaining part of this year, joy will be your portion in the name of Jesus! Amen! If the clothes of prisoners are being made with gold, you will not wear them in Jesus's name! If a coffin is sold for a dollar, you will not buy it in the name of Jesus!

I'm praying for somebody. I say, your best picture will not be used for your obituary in the name of Jesus!—no untimely death for you.

God is not a joker. He means business. When He draws you to Himself, He has a blessing that He wants to give to you. When you enter the presence of God with thanksgiving, He enters into your life with power.

Power to receive the dynamic ability that will cause changes that will make people want to serve your God because they have seen the great thing He has done in your life.

I will be speaking to you on what I call the power of attitude. The Lord has started preparing us for the upcoming year. I went before the Lord, and I was praying, and the Lord told me He had started preparing the church. He had started packaging glorious things. He said the upcoming year 2020 would be glorious, although the beginning might be rough and tough. It would be a year of double speed and protection. What kill others will not be able to kill you.

In this upcoming year, you would achieve what you had failed to achieve in the previous year in Jesus's name. When you think that by all circumstances, it is impossible, you are receiving it in the name of Jesus! According to the word of the Lord, which He said to me that a lot will perish, but those who trust in Him will fly on eagle's wings. They will run but never weary.

He said He will never disappoint those who trust in Him. He said that He will turn you around in 180 degrees. What people believe you cannot achieve, all those glories of the past that the devil had contested with you, the Lord is fighting your battle, and He is putting everything in your account in the name of Jesus! It's going to multiply you sevenfold in the name of Jesus!

The Lord asked me to give you this. He said that your attitude is like a price tag. It shows how valuable you are. In Genesis 20:13–21, when Joseph's brothers returned to him, they thought Joseph was going to kill them. But because of the good attitude of Joseph, he forgave them, and the Lord brought him to the highest point where no foreigner can be. In the land of Egypt, it has never been recorded that a foreigner rose to the position Joseph rose to. Even after his death, there hadn't been anyone. The same thing the Lord said is that He is going to visit someone here, and He will surprise you. You will look at yourself in the mirror and marvel because the Lord would have so decorated you, advanced you, shone His glory upon you, blessed and multiplied you in the name of Jesus!

A bad attitude is like a flat tire; if you don't change it, you will never get anywhere. Listen to me; any habit you form and you refuse to reform, it will one day deform you. And that is why God is giving this message. He is preparing your way because if you are not ready, you might remain on a spot for a long time, which I don't pray happens to anyone. I pray for success and glory for you in the coming year in the name of Jesus! It is your portion in the name of Jesus!

What is attitude?

Attitude is a settled way of thinking or feeling about something. That's your attitude. The pastor has given a lot of messages, but you said you will not change, that the pastor is just wasting his time every Sunday. The preacher is not wasting his time. He is only fulfilling the destiny God has given unto him. The ball is now in your court. If you heed to the voice of the Holy Spirit, you will receive the reward of heaven. And if you refuse the voice of God, there's also a reward for it, but it might not be palatable (Deuteronomy 28:1). The Bible made us understand that "if you listen diligently to the voice of the Lord to do all that I commanded you to do, then these blessings will come upon you and be your portion, but if you refuse," curses will not be your portion in the name of Jesus! Look at it, Vashti was a queen, and the king requested her to show herself to his guests; but she said no, that she was too beautiful to come to the palace and show her beauty to all the king's visitors. The king realized that it was pride preventing her from obeying his command, and she was immediately replaced by a younger woman, Esther. Your glory will not be given to someone else.

Listen to me and listen well. There are four attitudes that I would like you to watch out for. Please begin to watch out for it from this year because God will begin to supply to you new things from now till you enter into the New Year. And by the time you enter, God is going to speed it up. So there are four things the Lord is bringing your attention to from now.

1. *Your attitude to life.* You need to recognize that life is a gift. It is a privilege, not a right. You don't have any part to play before coming to this world. Nobody here can claim that he or she had any part to play before coming to this world. It's a desire of God that allowed you to come. You were already here before you realized it, so you never planned it, but God did. So your attitude to life this year is to give thanks to the person that planted you from the foundation. When you don't even know, He has planted you inside your mother's womb. You were not aware of your delivery, but God knew about it. So your attitude to life should be one of appreciation. This year you have to watch out for your attitude. Life is a gift. You must appreciate God for your life. No wonder Psalm 150:6 says "Let everything that has breath praise the Lord" because He is a faithful God. He spared your life. He knows you from the foundation even before you know yourself. Nobody has a part to play in coming to this world. You never instructed your father to marry your mother, did you? No! Your attitude to life this year is to appreciate Him that formed you in your mother's womb. Am I talking to somebody?

    You must realize that life is all about contribution, the purpose of this life. The reason you are alive is for you to contribute. And the day you stop contributing is the day you die.

It's a known fact that we have only two living things on earth, which are plants and animals. Those are the only two living things. Cars don't have life—houses and money likewise. God created these living things to contribute. God formed it in such a way that plants generate oxygen, which man needs to live because he cannot generate his own oxygen. but plants generate oxygen, give to man to use, and man, in return, gives out carbon dioxide for the plants to use to produce its food through the process of photosynthesis. Now listen to me; the day any of them stop producing these elements is the day they die. When God revealed these to me, I now figured out that in this life, the number one purpose of man is to value life and appreciate it. Anytime you stop helping people, that is the time God is turning His back on you. You are in this world to come and help no matter how little or big God made you to be a contributing factor. That is what you are designed for. And when you fail, you die. Contribute in everything—to help the church, wives to help the husbands, husbands to help their wives, children to help their parents and vice versa, and everyone to help somebody. To help individuals is tantamount to contributing your quota. Attitude to life is one of the things I want you to look out for to appreciate life.

No matter how stingy you are, you will still give out carbon dioxide; you cannot keep it to yourself. Life is about contribution, not consumption. It's about relevance, not significance. It's about service, not your status. It's about sacrifice, not supply. Life is all about giving and receiving. Acts 20:33–35 states that Jesus said that it is more blessed to give than to receive. Your attitude to life is to appreciate God and know fully well that you are contributing to someone's life while you are helping someone. God Himself is helping you.

2. *Attitude to God.* In Deuteronomy 6:4–6, it states, "Hear, O Israel; the Lord our God is one Lord, and thou shalt love the Lord thy God with all thine heart and with all thy soul.

And with all thy might and these words, which I command thee this day shall be in thy heart."

It says, "Hear, O Israel, the Lord your God is one." It stresses your attitude toward God. He is the mother of destiny. He is too big to require human support. God is just looking forward to your heart to know if you have a heart for Him so as to be able to bless you more. God needs nothing from anybody. When He gives you the opportunity to help somebody, He is enlarging your coast. When God assists you enough to assist someone, God is opening a channel for you to expand more. When God gives you the opportunity to help His church, it's a big avenue for your enlargement. In the upcoming year, please, I implore you to take all these things into account. When you assume a supportive attitude toward God with pride, He turns His back at you. "I am the one supporting that church." Hmm. God will be moved to raise people of humble beginnings, and they will begin to do exploits. When you are helping others, you are actually helping yourself. You are preparing your table. It is not how much you save that amounts to your prosperity; it is the number of blessings upon the little you have. You need to appreciate that the totality of your existence is a product of His grace. You are what you are by His grace. You are in this place not because of your connection or education but because God loves to move you to a better level to enjoy His divine grace. Alleluia to the Son of the living God. When you appreciate God for the little you got, then He gives you His presence. And once you have a divine presence, it is the greatest asset in the race of life. When God is with you, there's nothing that can be more valuable than that.

God was with Abraham at seventy-five years old. And from ninety-nine years old, God turned his bareness to a gift of many nations. God was with Joseph. He removed him from the prison straight to the palace. God was with Moses before he parted the red sea, and the Israelites walked on dry ground. God was with David, and he brought Goliath down with a swing of his catapult. God was with Joshua, and he told the sun to stand still during the battle at Aijalon, and all his enemies were destroyed. When you are with God. He is the greatest asset any man can have in the race of life. In Romans 8:31, it states, "If God be for us, who can be against us." It is not possible for you to carry God and be a failure. If you are struggling with life, it might be because you had never allowed God to step in fully into your case. If you allow Him, your story changes; and people will marvel at your God.

3. *Your attitude to work.*

Abide in me and I in you. As the branch cannot bear fruit of itself except it abide in the vine; no more can ye, except ye abide in me. John 15:4–5

Work is not a curse. "Abide in me and I in you." God is telling you that in order for you to be fruitful and productive in the coming year, you need to abide in Christ. Your attitude to work should not be that of a slave. The Bible says that whatsoever your hands find to do, do it. Your job is what you are trained to do. Your work is what you are divinely wired to do. Many times, you need your job to be able to get to your work. Are you listening to me? You need your job first. And from there, you will advance to your own work because your work is what you have a natural endowment for, something that is in built, something God has deposited in you. that is your work, while your job is what you are trained to do. So when you are at your job, make sure you walk yourself up to your work. Work is not a curse, rather it is a channel of blessing designed by God for your destiny to shine. Nothing happens until you make it happen. If you are waiting for a better day, a better day doesn't come by itself. You have to work at it. A better day is now. Don't fold your arms and wait. No, set it before the

Lord in prayer and work it out. And if God is with you, He will open your path, and success will be yours.

Everything big today started small. The Bible says, "Do not despise the day of humble beginnings." Someone owns where you are working right now. Start and set a plan for yourself. Commit it to God in prayers, and He will begin to guide you. And before you know it, *boom*!

This morning, when I was driving to church, it just came to me. When I started this church, I already rented a place and gave out fliers, but I conducted the first service all by myself. I preached to the tables and chairs, yet nobody showed up until two people joined. Then gradually God began to bring wonderful people to me, people God already promised the movers and shakers of their society. If you are one of the movers and shakers, shout alleluia! *Hallelujah*!

You have to change your attitude to work. You need to work, rest, and serve the Lord. You need to plan everything out. You cannot be lazy and expect manna from heaven. God does not bless people with money. He only sends blessings because it is the blessings of the Lord that make rich and add no sorrow (Proverbs 10:22). You need to have a positive attitude of leadership and know fully well that this employer is privileged to have you, and in no distant future, you will be hiring people.

Any training you acquire in your job should be invested in your work. That's why we go to school. Whatever we learn in school is translated into knowledge and wisdom to benefit us. I have these long-term friends; two of them started a business some years back. But now, the business has expanded. That's why you have to start something. Look at what King David said in Psalm 78:72: "So he fed them according to the integrity of his heart, and guided them by the skillfulness of his hand." David was so skillful in what he did. He played guitar so very well. So when the spirit of madness fell upon King Saul, they looked for him to play his instrument, and the spirit of madness left the king. Eventually, he became the king. What are you good at?

4. *Attitude to money.* Listen to me. Money is simply a medium of exchange. money is only a blessing. If you have it, it becomes a curse if it has you. When money is the one controlling you, you are under a curse. Am I talking to somebody? Money in your hands is a blessing. But when it gets to your heart, it becomes a curse. Money is placed in your hands to enhance your stewardship of the world, not just to enlarge your possession. Let me tell you how to test your heart because many people will be wondering if their heart is focused on heaven or earth. Whenever you make some money or you have time, where do you spend it? Whenever you get your paycheck, what comes to your mind first? Do you think about investing in the gospel like tithes, offerings, or radio or television evangelism? Or do you think about giving back to society in the form of homeless, motherless orphanages versus thinking of buying more clothes and watches to show off class. Did you thank the Lord for the increment, or do you brag about your expertise?

You will discover that some people from January to December don't have any reason to thank God. All they do is murmur and complain all through the year. Whenever you complain, you remain on the same spot. But when you praise, you are raised. That's how it works.

If you haven't given your life to Christ, this is another opportunity to become a child of God. Give the totality of your life to God. You are still contesting your time with God. If you haven't surrendered everything to God, please have a change of heart and turn to God now.

Say this prayer after me:

Lord Jesus, I come to you today. I accept you as my Lord and personal Savior. I forsake all my sins. Satan, I depart from you and all your work. Jesus, I embrace you, and I want you to dwell in me. Thank You for saving me in Jesus's name. Amen.

If you prayed that prayer, I welcome you to the kingdom of God. The Lord has written your name in the Lamb's book of record. Amen.

Let us pray. Almighty and invisible God, you are the only wise God. Unto you we come today. Father, you have given us instructions on our attitude this year. Please, our Lord and our God, help us monitor our attitude and align it with your character in the name of Jesus. If there be anywhere we are about to derail, please put us back in line in the name of Jesus. If there be anywhere we fell, Father, please lift us up in the name of Jesus. Let your grace sustain us forever in the name of Jesus! Thank You, Lord, because you have answered this prayer. In Jesus's mighty name, we pray. Amen!

12/22/2019
THE TEST OF A TRUE FOLLOWER OF JESUS CHRIST

> Then said Jesus unto his disciples. If any man will come after me, let him deny himself and take up his cross and follow me. (Matthew 16:24)
>
> And ye shall seek me and find me, when ye shall search for me with all your heart. (Jeremiah 29:13)

The Lord is working wonders in your life. If you believe, please, can you stand up and share the testimony with others? Please share it with faith. He is working wonders in the name of Jesus. Amen!

I will be talking to you today on what I call the test of a true follower of Jesus Christ. Today I came to church with a tester to test you, brethren, on the positive side, whether you weigh less or more. I have the spiritual tester that the Lord has given me today to bring to church before we close this year and step into another year. I want you to ask yourself a rhetorical question. A rhetorical question is one that is asked without the intent of an answer. Ask your inner mind, "Am I a true follower of Jesus Christ?" You don't need to answer now. The answer will come to you by itself. You don't need to think about the answer. It is neither yes nor no. the answer itself will come to you before the end of today's message.

The God that we serve is a self-sufficient God. He is too big to require human help or assistance. He doesn't need man for anything, but man needs Him for all things. Anything He didn't do remains undone till eternity. And anything he did is done forever. Nothing shall be taken away or added to it (Ecclesiastes 3:14).

It is His will to do what He is doing. It is His will to give you the gift of life. It is His will to open doors for you. It is His will to suppress your enemies with defeat. It is His will to elevate you. It is His will to exalt you. It is His will to give you comfort. It is His will to bless you. It is His will to prosper you. It is His will to make you live long. It is His will to make you see your grandchildren. I hope I am talking to someone today. Alleluia to the Son of the living God!

Anytime I wake up and see myself alive, I check my body and say to myself that "the lion is up today. Let the enemies tremble." Can you shout out, "Let the enemies tremble!" When the lion rises up in the morning, he gives thanks to Almighty God, and its only prayer is, "Father, show me the animal you want me to eat. Don't help me to catch it. Please just point it out to me so if I cannot catch it, then it's left to me." I am equal to the task, and you know when the lion roars one mile to that place, every animal that hears its roaring begins to fidget because the king of the jungle has just spoken. Is there anyone here that is the prince of Jesus that can shout and tell the world, "Let my enemy be quiet forever!"

Anything you want to see, you have to say. A Hollywood star said something, and he is correct. He said, 'If you want to be a star, act like one." Anything you cannot profess, you cannot possess. If you can't say it out, you can possess it. If you can't see it, God can't give it. You need to be able to see it before God can give it to you (Genesis 13:14–15). You are going into a glorious destiny in Jesus's name. God will fulfill all your heart's desires in the name of Jesus!

Obedience to the commandment of Jesus Christ is a sure way to a true test of the follower of Jesus Christ. The only sure way you can know whether you are a true follower is to obey His commandments. You cannot see Jesus. He is not here in person. He has ascended into heaven, but He left His words with us, and your compliance with the word is a sure way to know that you are following Him. Each of us complies with the laid-down principles and standards of the country we all live in. That is why we can live well wherever we are. Also, in the kingdom of God, if you comply with the laws of the kingdom of God, that is what makes you know that, for sure, you are a follower of Jesus Christ. And Jesus said this in John 14:15, "If ye love me" those of you that claim to love Jesus, the test is coming, He is telling you to "keep my commandment." Jesus is giving us an instruction here that the only way He knows is that if you love Him, it is not the money you bring to church; it is not the children you are raising, rather the house you built. It is not all those things you do religiously; it is when you comply with His commandment.

Loving one another is what Jesus declares, and it is the greatest of all the laws. Jesus Christ Himself categorizes all these laws and His instructions and rated love the greatest of all. Mathew 22:35–40 states, "Then one of them which was a lawyer asked Him a question tempting Him and said, Master which is the greatest commandment in the law? Jesus said unto Him, thou shalt love the Lord thy God with all thy heart, and thy soul and thy mind. And this is the first and great commandment and the second is like unto it thou shalt love thy neighbor as thyself." If you fulfill all these, you fulfill all the commandments. Alleluia!

Love is expressed in our ability to make up for our differences. Love is measured by the degree of sacrifice you are ready to give. For many of us, our spouses might not be the ideal ones; but you sacrifice your life. You overlook all the shortcomings, and love prevailed over all other circumstances. And you said to him/her, "I do." Your family members might oppose the relationship, but the love you got solidifies the union. And you say, "I do," and you journey together. There is no secret between you. Why?—because of love. Sometimes when our children do something wrong, we tend to get mad and yell at them. But after some time we, let it go because of the love we have for our children, which is inborn. The mother helps her child rise up when he/she falls through her own life experience. But fathers don't do that. They teach their child through the experiences of others. Your mother will guide you from falling. Fathers don't do that. They allow you to fall and guide you on how to rise again. Mothers will try to prevent you from falling. You do all these because of the love you have for your children. That is why I said that love is measured by the degree of sacrifice you are willing to make.

Jesus washed the feet of His disciples (Luke 26:14–39) as a sign of humility. He bent down to wash the dirtiest part of the body of His disciples. Peter did not want Him to wash his feet, but Jesus said, "If you did not allow me to wash your feet, you will not have a part in my kingdom." He knelt down. Jesus knelt down and washed His disciples' legs one after the other as a sign of love He has shown to the world. In John 13:34, Jesus said, "A new commandment I give unto you that ye love one another." Jesus did not say love me, but love one another as I have loved you. So when you love one another, that is when Jesus knows that you truly love Him. Alleluia!

If you love with the love of Christ, that is when He knows you as His follower. If you backbite against a sister, brother, pastor, or any brethren, you are going against the will of Christ. You are failing the test. It is the love you show to your neighbor that shows how much you love Jesus. Your service is in vain if you don't love your neighbor. That's how the Bible puts it. There's a need for you to love. I'm not talking about friendship. Friendship is a choice, but love is mandatory, especially for those of us in the same household of faith. Remember, we were of different backgrounds. We were raised differently. You cannot expect everybody to be behave. And I say to you, it is the degree by which you can make up the differences that makes you a child of God. Paul the apostle said, "Forgive penitent for the sake of himself and forgive impenitent for the sake of heaven." What was he saying? He said you should forgive anybody that offends you and comes to apologize for the sake of himself, and impenitent is someone who offended you and never apologized. Paul said to forgive such a person for the sake of heaven.

Forgiveness is a gift you give to yourself. It is also a sign of the follower of Christ even if the person is tormenting you, getting on your nerves. Yours is to show love because Christ is in you, and you cannot do less, not that you are pretending about it. No! You cannot pretend more than a month on any issues because life is too short to keep expressing anger.

As a follower of Christ:

1. *Make love your priority.* First John 3:11 states, "For this is the Message that ye heard from the beginning to love one another." Love one another. Husband, love your wife. Wife, respect your husband. Choir members, respect your leaders. Honor and value yourself. There are bound to be differences. But when you are able to make up for the differences, you exhibit love. Every love, response, and act of goodwill must first pass through the divine filter of love. Everything you do in this kingdom must pass that filter of love. If you fail the test of love, there's no reward for it. You must know that loving your neighbor is a demand of Jesus Christ. Love is the only virtue that cannot fail. It is a failure-proof virtue. Every other thing will fail, but love never fails. First Corinthians 13:8 states, "Charity (love) never fails." Whatever you do in the name of love, Jesus is coming back to pay you. God established love as the impetus for obedience.
2. *Embody the distinguished nature of love.* The Bible says by this love, and Jesus Christ said by this love, that all the people will know that you are my disciple. It is not by preaching or prayer that people will know that you are my disciple. But if you love one another, it is by this love. It is not by your effort in the church. It is not by the big donations you make either, but by love. John 13:35 states, "By this shall all men know that you are my disciple if ye have love one to another." If you turn it around, it says that by this shall all men know that you are not my disciple if you hate one another.

Who do you hate and why? What is the basis of the hatred? Why can't we embrace ourselves for the sake of Christ? This is the best time we have to reconcile. A time is coming that the wife will turn her back to the husband and say goodbye. The same goes for the man. Paul the apostle said, "Let me suffer loss for the sake of God so that I can gain someone into the kingdom of heaven." Let's lift our hands toward heaven and begin to pray, heavenly Father, let your love take hold of my life in the name of Jesus in every way, every circumstance. Open your mouth and begin to decree it.

When a member of our church was about to lose his house. I was away on a trip. Some church elders gathered together and came up with the amount of money needed to restore him back to his house. That is what I call the love of Christ. Alleluia!

The plan of God from the beginning was to develop a people that reflected His character and what His character is: love.

> And we have known and believed the love that God hath to us. God is love and he that dwelleth in love dwelleth in God and God in him. Herein is our love made perfect, that we may have boldness in the day of judgment; because as he is so are we in this world. (1 John 4:16–17)

Demonstrating the virtue of love

How can we practice the glorious virtue of love?

1. *Love values the other person.* Let's not confuse Christianity. Love with its modern counterfeits—lust, sentimentality, and gratification—while love is a wonderful, warm feeling. It is not only a feeling. In fact, according to the Bible, love is primarily an active interest in the well-being of another person. Love acts for the benefit of others. According to the scripture, love is a fruit of spirit (Galatians 5:22–23). And as you express love, the father is glorified, and you bear much fruit.

Jesus told a parable.

> A certain man went down from Jerusalem to Jericho and fell among thieves, which stripped

him of his raiment and wounded him, and departed, leaving him half dead. And by chance there came down a certain priest that way and when he saw him, he passed by on the other side. And likewise a Levite when he was at the place came and looked on him and passed by on the other side. But a certain Samaritan as he journeyed, came where he was and when he saw him, he had compassion on him And went to him and bound up his wounds, pouring in oil and wine and set him on his beast and brought him to an inn and took care of him. And on the morrow when he departed, he took out two pence and gave them to the host and said unto him, Take care of him and whatsoever thou spendest more when I come again I will repay thee Which now of these three thinkest thou, was neighbour unto him that fell among the thieves. And he said, He that shewed mercy on him. Then said Jesus unto him. Go and do thou likewise. (Luke 10:30–37)

2. *Love is vulnerable to others.* We cannot love others like Christ without Christ. He left the glory of heaven and came to earth. He veiled His divinity and took on humanity.

    Being generous—that is, giving freely of yourself, your time, and your energy—kindles vulnerability. Generosity is an outward expression of sensitivity and compassion for your partner. The empathy and understanding that are fundamental to being truly generous also sustain the vulnerability of both the giver and the receiver. When an act of generosity grows out of this type of attunement to and appreciation of your partner's uniqueness, it gratifies both of you. So if you truly love, you will accept some challenges because of who you love.

3. *Love entails a cost.* The measure of our maturity is our love for God and love for others. If we fail in our love, we have missed what it means to be a follower of Christ.

    True love is not free. When we are truly in love with someone, we are willing to pay for that love with much more than silver and gold. Love is not a commodity to be bought, sold, and traded, but it is a precious energy that costs us our life force.

12/24/2019
THE ESSENCE OF CHRISTMAS

> For unto us a child is born, unto us a son is given and the government shall be upon his shoulder; and his name shall be called Wonderful, Counsellor, The mighty God, The everlasting father, The Prince of peace. (Isaiah 9:6)

> And the angel said unto them, Fear not for behold I bring you good tidings of great joy, which shall be to all people. For unto you is born this day in the city of David a saviour, which is Christ the Lord And this shall be a sign unto you, ye shall find the babe wrapped in swaddling clothes, lying in a manger. (Luke 2:10–12)

There's no way to go to heaven except through Jesus Christ. Habakkuk 1:13 said, "God has a purer eye that cannot behold iniquity."

Our forefathers had sinned, and it has been transferred to all the human race (adamic nature). Because of this, no one can enter into the presence of God (Habakkuk 1:13) or receive eternal life anymore. Then Jesus Christ decided to come into the world to suffer for an offense He never committed. He suffered so that you and I will never have to suffer. He endured the cross so that we will never have to endure any shame anymore. And the Bible is telling us today in Isaiah 9:6, "For unto us a child is born." To the world, a baby that was born is a child. But in the same verse, look at it: "But unto us a Son is given." There is a difference between a child and a son. When you give birth to a little baby, it's a child. But when you nurture that child, and he grows to do great and mighty person, you no longer call him a child but rather a son. So God is telling us in this verse that to us, He is a child; but to Him, He is a Son of God that was given to us—God's incarnate.

God stepped out of Himself to produce Himself to come to this world for the remission of our sins.

Things Jesus did for us. He came to raise us as victorious people. That is one lesson I want us to take home today. You are not under any curse. Don't allow anyone to deceive you that it is the curse of your father or mother's lineage that is tormenting you. If you are genuinely born again, you cannot be under any curse. Therefore, if any man is in Christ, he is a new creature. Old things have passed away, and everything has become new (2 Corinthians 5:17). You are a newborn child of God. You are not under any curse. Galatians 3:13–14 states, "Christ has redeemed us from the curse of the law being made a curse for us for it is written cursed is everyone that was hanged on the tree that the blessing of Abraham might come to the Gentiles through Jesus Christ; that we might receive the promise of the spirit through faith."

Don't allow anyone to deceive you. You cannot be under any curse unless you are not genuinely born again. Don't allow anyone to put you under any curse because Jesus is enough to save you, and He has saved you (verse 26). You are entitled to the salvation Christ gives. That is the lesson I want you to take home today. You might be struggling with some situations and conditions. Yes, the Bible says, "In the world there will be tribulations but be of good cheer because I have overcome the world" (John 16:33). There may be ups and downs; there are some mountains that you need to climb; but when you overcome the mountain, you become a master over the problem. These little things that come your way are to make you strong in the Lord. If there was no Goliath in the life of David, he would never amount to a king forever. That was how he got recognized. If there's a little challenge on your way, God wants to elevate you.

I told someone some time ago that troubles and problems are university of advancement. When it comes your way, endure it, struggle through it, move forward, call Jesus, and He will walk you through it, and you will overcome it forever. If there was no Red Sea in the path of the Israelites, they would never get to Canaan land. The Red Sea would come and go, then the promised land is the next.

Every problem that comes to you as a believer, the end result of it will give glory to God. Amen! Let's lift our hands toward heaven and declare that we are not under any curse, that we are free indeed. Jesus Christ came into this world to set us free. Open your mouth, and declare your freedom in the name of Jesus.

Almighty and ever-loving God, you are so good to us. Thank You, King of glory, for bringing us to Yourself today and for the manna for which You fed us. Let Your words we hear today germinate and sow seeds in our lives in the name of Jesus! Father, we don't want to be speakers or hearers alone, deceiving ourselves. We want to be doers of Your word with the ability to continue doing Your word. Father, release it unto us in the name of Jesus. Thank You, Lord, because You have answered this prayer. In Jesus's mighty name we pray. Amen!

12/29/2019
POWER OF THANKSGIVING

> Oh, give thanks to God for He is good for his mercy endureth for ever. (Psalm 107:1)

God has all the power. He has all the authority and knowledge. There's no power that is more than Him. There's no ability that Surpass His own. He knows all things and can do all things. He knows yesterday. He is the only God that can go to your yesterday to readjust or repair yesterday. He is the only God that can move from yesterday to today. No other being can do that except Jehovah Jireh. He is the only one that can go to tomorrow before it is tomorrow. He is our God. He is our maker. He has all the wisdom. He is a pathfinder, a waymaker. He has all the authority in heaven and on earth. Whatever He says is final. He consults nobody. He depends on nobody. He relies on nobody, but the whole world relies on Him. He is the ancient of days, the I Am that I Am. He is Jehovah Tisdkenu, Jehovah Rapha. Alleluia to the Son of God! That God is working miracles in your life today in the name of Jesus!

We serve a wonderful Jesus. His name is El Shaddai, Lord God Almighty, Elohim, the Most High God, Adonai, Lord Master, Yahweh, Lord Jehovah, Jehovah Nissi, the Lord my banner, Jehovah Rapha, the Lord my shepherd, the Lord my healer, Jehovah Shammah, the Lord is there, Jehovah Tsidkenu, the Lord is our righteousness, Jehovah Jireh, the Lord is my provider, Jehovah Shalom, the Lord is my peace, and Jehovah Saboti. The awesome God, the Father of all—that is the God we serve, and that God is doing wonders in your life today in the name of Jesus!

I want you to think deep in your heart and think of what God has done for you. When you acknowledge God for what He has done, you propel Him to do more. If God has done something, and you fail to appreciate Him because you were expecting Him to do more than what He did, you might experience some delay because you failed to appreciate the little He did initially. Appreciating Him will open more doors of joy for you. We need to appreciate God in all things, in every circumstance, and condition. Give yourself a pause at times. Stop wining. Stop murmuring. Even the gift of life in itself alone is enough to give Him praise. The first miracle that can happen to anyone on a daily basis is the gift of life. When you wake up in the morning, and you see yourself standing. A lady ran crazy immediately after she gave birth to a baby boy in the hospital. Can you imagine how many babies you gave birth to, but you stayed healthy after delivery? She was fine before she went to the labor room. But immediately after, a problem arose. She is still in that mental illness up till now. Doctors have no solution to her problem. They gave her medications daily, but her condition did not improve. It is worth glorifying God, to say thank You, Jesus! Father Lord, we appreciate You. May the Lord accept our thanksgiving.

What about feeding? Not everyone can feed themselves. Don't you see people when you travel or go around? Don't you see beggars on the streets? They were born like you and me, but God has highly favored you. Do not condition yourself based on any particular situation you find yourself in. That is not all, God has done a lot for you that you ought to be thankful for. Alleluia!

WHY MUST WE THANK GOD? God is good and His mercies endure forever. Thank God because He is good. If God is not good, many of us will not be alive. Many of us have done things, which we ought not to have done. Many of us trespassed that God was supposed to have cut us off, but because of the goodness of God, your life is still preserved. Many witches and wizards don't want you to sleep and see the light of a new day; but because of the goodness of God, He sent His guardian angels to you. While you are sleeping, they watch over you to cut off any evil spirit around your abode with the sword of Angel Michael. But when you wake up in the morning, you think it's by your strength, not knowing it was the power of God that protected you through the perils of the night. Psalm 136:1 says, "Oh, give thanks to the Lord for He is good and His mercies endureth forever." Before our forefathers, He has been God. Long after we are gone, He will still be God, and people will still be worshipping Him. We are privileged to serve and worship Him.

Number two reason why we must thank God: He kept us above the ground. Psalm 41:2 states, "The Lord will preserve him and keep Him alive and he shall be blessed upon the land and thou will not deliver him into the will of his enemies." What is the will of the enemy? The will of the enemy is that you sleep and never wake up. The will of the enemy is that you never make a headway in life. But the Bible says that God will not allow the wish of the enemy to come upon your life. That will be your story in the name of Jesus! Amen!

In Psalm 145:15–16, the Bible made us understand that "every eyes look upon the Lord and the Lord give them their bread in due season." it is the Lord that is paying your house rent. It is the Lord that is paying your mortgage, your car note. It is the Lord that is feeding you. It is the Lord that is sustaining everyone living (Deuteronomy 8:18). Every morning, the Bible says that the hands full of God pour onto the earth; and every creature eats from there, including animals and plants. Everything living eats from the hands full of God. It is God that feeds you, not your work. You are positioned in that place of work to bless the place, and the blessings of God will be your portion in the name of Jesus!

Number three, why we need to thank God is because God is building His church. In Matthew 16:18, God was sustaining His own church. He said, "I will build my church, and the gate of hell will never prevail over it." The wish of the wicked ones is that this church will come to ruins. But because it is found by the instructions of the Holy Spirit, nothing can destroy it forever. Am I talking to somebody? The foundation remains sure because it was built by God Himself.

Do you know one thing? God is not happy when you murmur. Many of you still remain where you are because you complain a lot. Let me show you two scriptural passages that may inspire you to stop murmuring.

> Neither murmur ye like some of them also murmured and were destroyed by destroyer. (1 Corinthians 10:10)

When you praise God, He will raise you from any dungeon, trouble, sickness. He will raise you. But when you murmur, God will send a destroyer to destroy you. There is no shortcut. If you shortcut, you will cut short.

> And when the people complained it displeased the Lord and the Lord heard it and His anger was kindled and the fire of the Lord burnt among them and consumed them that were in the uttermost part of the camp. (Numbers 11:1)

God destroyed them by fire because they complained from January to December. You might be looking for one thing but haven't gotten it. Don't complain; but rather, praise God. There's a reason why God is keeping it away from you. This upcoming year, one thing I want you to do is to be focused. If you need a change of story, you have a part to play in the solution to your problem. You can't fold your hands and complain. No! You have to praise, set a goal for yourself and focus on it, put in prayer, and work toward it. There's nothing difficult that you set before the Lord that He will not give to you in the name of Jesus. You will witness a change of story in the name of Jesus! I see the upcoming year, a fantabulous one for us in the name of Jesus! God will open doors that no man can close. If there is any government that wants to stand in your way, the Lord will replace them in the name of Jesus!

Let's rise up. Lift your hands toward heaven and begin to declare, Father, I give You praise. I thank You for the wonderful things You are doing in my life, Father. This year, Lord, I want to be focused. I want to walk with You. I want you to work through me. Open Your mouth and declare it in the name of Jesus. My God and my Father, let this year be a good turning point in my life, a time of joy, elevation, a time of advancement in the name of Jesus. Thank You, King of glory, because You have answered. In Jesus's mighty name, we pray. Amen.

01/01/2020
DIVINE DIRECTION

In the upcoming year, there's going to be a debate over your life. There's going to be divine transformation and transportation and transmogrification. There's going to be a wealth transfer. The Lord is going to convert the abundance of ocean into your pocket in the name of Jesus. Alleluia to the Son of the living God!

In this year that you enter, you will not sweat too much before you have results and substantial amounts of blessing in the name of Jesus! The era of labor, labor, and labor before you eat is over. You have stepped into an era of favor, favor, and favor in the name of Jesus. The Lord is on our side. Like a mighty warrior, every gang up of the enemy upon your life, you will hear of their obituary. Enough is enough. Anywhere they conspire evil, Michael the archangel from heaven will pierce them with his sword in the name of Jesus!

This year, you are not only looking for a job, rather you are hiring. What you are going to accomplish this year is not based on your effort; it will be based on who He is. It is not going to answer your name but *His* name. According to what He said to the children of Israel, "I will bring you out of slavery for my namesake, not because of your righteousness, not because of your effort but for my namesake and the namesake of my Son, Jesus Christ." He will deliver fortune into your hand this year in the name of Jesus!

In the journey of life, effort and courage are not enough without divine purpose and divine direction. Divine direction is the maker of stars. It is whom the Lord is helping. It is not color, race, position, credentials, height, depth, connection, gender. It is whom the Lord is helping. This year, the Lord will lead you, and the Lord will help you. No wonder David said, "He led me in the path of righteousness for His namesake." This year, you will not make irrational decisions. You will not take decisions that will end you in jail. You will not take decisions that will end your life untimely. You won't take such decisions in the name of Jesus! You shall be protected from global sickness and diseases. This year, you will not walk by yourself without being accomplished by the Holy Spirit. You will not struggle by yourself. You will have the Almighty God beside you to accomplish everything for you for His namesake in the name of Jesus.

Divine direction brings God into your big decision.

> Thirsteth not, when He led them through the desert, He caused the water to flow out of the rock for them, the cave and the rock also, the water gushed out. (Isaiah 48:21)

Look at all those people in the wilderness. The Bible says they thirst not because the Lord is leading them. God supplied all they needed. They had no farm, and the Lord was feeding them every day. In the day, the Lord turned Himself into a cloud to shield them from the heat of the sun. In the night the Lord turned Himself into a pillar of fire to warm them up and give them light for forty solid years. That is the same God that will lead you this year. Anywhere you go this year, don't go by yourself. Any of your documents submitted, any application you fill, don't fill it by your connection or power of your credentials, but submit it in the name of the Lord. Let the name of the Lord accompany it. Nobody rejects God. You will never be rejected in the name of Jesus! Your decision is not enough. You need divine empowerment. You have to bring God into your story. Enough of your struggling. You have done it your own way, but it's obviously not working.

A man was working on a business. According to him, he had tried all his connections. He had used all his money to try and see if the business would bounce back, all to no avail. He sought the face of God in prayer and served the Lord, and the doors opened for him.

This year, you will not be a project for a fake pastor. Think about that prayer, brethren. Anything you decide to do for God, do it willingly with faith. Paul the apostle said that it has to be willfully for God to open the window and doors of heaven for you (1 Corinthians 9:17). Many times, you need a sacrifice on the altar of thanksgiving before God (Deuteronomy 16:16). Look at King Solomon. Instead of one lamb, he brought one thousand lambs to God for an offering. God commanded the Israelites to bring just one lamb (2 Chronicle 1:6, 1 Kings 3:4), but Solomon said, "God has done great things in his life, and he brought a thousand." That same night, God descended from heaven, woke him up, and said, "Solomon, because you have done this for me, ask me anything." And Solomon asked for wisdom to lead his people. God told him, "Wisdom—you will have it. But in prosperity and in wealth, no king will be like you. No king will be compared to your level of prosperity after you." The richest person on earth cannot be matched with King Solomon in wealth and wisdom, even the wealthiest man on earth till date. You are reaching that level in the name of Jesus. The Lord will empower you and bring financial prosperity to you in the name of Jesus.

Divine direction is the key to an unending breakthrough when God is leading you. You will experience a breakthrough on every side. No wonder Proverbs 4:18 says, "The path of a just man is like a shining light that shines more and more unto the perfect day of the Lord." I say this to you, you will never experience a better last year in the name of Jesus. It will be from glory to glory, from honor to honor, in the name of Jesus!

In Jeremiah 10:23, it states, "Oh Lord, I know that the way of man is not in himself, it is not in man that waited and worketh to direct his path." So you can take the decision that you think is the best. The Bible says, there's a way that seems right in the face of men, but the end thereof is a way of perdition (Proverbs 14:12). So Jeremiah is telling you that, yes, you are planning, but your way is in the hands of your maker, not in you. And He is the one that will direct you where to go. When God is directing you, it will lead you to unending breakthroughs on every side. The value of a dollar is not determined in the stores. The value is determined from the mint where it was manufactured. They wrote a dollar on it. So whatever happens to the dollar in circulation? Maybe someone trampled on it, molested it, rubbished it, rubbed it in the mud, poured oil or soup on it. When you pick it up and take it to the store, it still remains a dollar. Nobody can say. Because there's an oil stain on it, the value has been reduced to fifty cents. No, it remains one dollar. Whatever happened to your life, maybe someone molested you, harassed you, ignored you, but when you rise up again, your glory will shine in the name of Jesus! Amen! Your glory and value have been predetermined by your Creator, not your spouse, not your boss. If you call someone your boss, it's a sign of respect to that person because you are too honorable to have a boss. You have only one boss, and He is in heaven. God is your boss. Am I really talking to somebody? When you get to your work, work diligently. Do not be lazy. Discharge your duties accordingly. If they fired you, it means God is pushing you to a better place because many of us don't want to move. Even when God wants to move you and you refuse to move, God will send someone to kick you out, and then you are fired. And God now takes you to your place of glory.

A lady was working in one of the cloth stores in town. She was hired during the holiday period. After the season was over, the boss told her she was fired. This lady went home crying, thinking all hope was lost. Out of the blues, a man came with his two children to drop them off with the babysitter. Per adventure, he met this lady in this apartment building. She happened to have met him before. After they got to talking, this man told the lady to apply to his organization that they were in urgent need of someone with her skills in mathematics. This lady did as she was told, and miraculously, she was sent to head the branch of that company in another state. God will kick you to your place of glory this year. So when they lie against you or fire you at work unjustly, call on God and tell your pastor to intercede for you in prayer. Don't cry. God has sent a step to move you up. The Lord is promoting you this year in the name of Jesus.

How does God direct?

1. *God directs by His word (Psalm 107:20).* Make the Bible your friend. I cannot overemphasize it. I appeal to you in the name of Jesus. There's no other way. There's no other power under heaven that can stand the Word of God. This is the living God. This is His Word. Make it your friend! Read it in the morning, noon, and night. Make sure you meditate, and God will direct you through His word. Most times, when I wake up in the morning to study the Bible, it directs me on what to do that day. It will tell me what will happen that day.

    Temptations will come. But if you study the Bible, you will not fall prey to it. Please, men and brethren, as you journey with God in this New Year, run away from women that are not yours. Five minutes of enjoyment will give you twenty-one years of sorrow. That will not be your portion. Be a decent ambassador of Christ. I want to see you step into your glory this year. Whatever it takes humanly possible, be it fasting, prayer because right from the time of John the Baptist, the kingdom of God suffereth violence and violence men taketh it by force

2. *God directs with His spirit (2 Corinthians 3:17).* Whenever the Spirit of God gives an instruction, please listen to it. There's a spirit within and a spirit upon. The spirit upon is for service, and when you come to church like this, it is the spirit upon that is working. There's a spirit within that follows you everywhere you go. It guides you to fortune. In Revelation 1:10, he said, When the spirit enter into me I heard who was talking to me and He put me on my feet to walk." If you want to work, you need the spirit of God to enter into you so that He can put you on your feet. Listen to this, all you spiritualist. If God did not send any message through you. Don't deceive the people of God and go to hell. Listen to what God said. He said, "Your light will I quench in gross darkness" (Job 18:5–6). The

Lord said, "I will combat you as an enemy." In the book of Jeremiah, God said He will be an enemy to those spiritualists deceiving His people. If your earthly father cursed you, you can go to your spiritual father who will avert the curse. If your spiritual father curses you, you can go to your heavenly Father to avert the curse. But if your heavenly Father cursed you, whom will you go to avert the curse on people! All those pastors saying "Thus saith the Lord" when the Lord has not spoken might be living in luxury today, I say to you, their sorrow is waiting for them soon.

Let this year be a serious year. Make the Bible your friend. Listen to your spirit within you and match it with the Spirit of God in the Bible. If you want God to direct you, you have to be born again. Until you are born again, you are in the synagogue and wilderness of the dead. You don't have any record with God. You are dead to life until you are born again. And how can you be born again?—until you accept Jesus Christ as your Lord and personal Savior.

Church is even not included. That is why I love God so much. He is not going to judge this world based on the garment you wear or denomination. It is not a license to get to heaven or hell. That is why we don't lay emphasis on cloth in our church. God is not judging based on these criteria. There's no church in heaven, only an assembly of the holies. If you are holy, you are a member of the church and there's no pastor in heaven Jesus Christ is the Priest. When you get to heaven there's no separation. Some ministers will be nowhere near the throne of grace. Some assistant pastors will be found wanting in heaven, while church members will be with a golden crown on their heads. People value some pastors in this world more than God. It's good to respect your pastor, but you don't have to worship him when he is doing something that is not right. You can correct him. It is a sign of love. That way, he won't fall by the wayside. This year, you are moving forward. No impediment will stop you in the name of Jesus! Be born again, and be filled with the Spirit of God. let's rise up for prayer.

01/05/2020
VISION 2020

The Bible says, "Who is the man that saith and come to pass when the Lord has not decreed it" (Lamentation 3:37). God has decreed to us that this year is the year of our glory and honor. I believe that you are so confident to proclaim to yourself that it is your year of glory and honor. So shall it be in the mighty name of Jesus. When you are confident enough to say it to yourself, you will be able to come out boldly in the face of the principalities of this world and also share the testimony with people.

Everything you had been expecting the Lord to bring to you in the name of Jesus! The Lord is making ways for us where there is no way. Declare it to yourself. I have a joy in me, which remains in every circumstance, because I have the King of kings, the Lord of lords backing me up, the Lord that installs kings in the absence of kingmakers. He doesn't consider or consult anyone to make a decision on my issue. Not even the government of your country can influence His decision on you, neither does He consider your past to determine your future. He doesn't consider the faults of my parents. He opens before showing me, one by one, a path that no one can block—the path of progress, salvation, joy, and abundance that is going to be your portion in the name of Jesus!

The theme of my message today is what I call vision 2020. This year 2020 is not just fun. You are privileged to know this year. Year 3030 will come too. But maybe, few of us will still be here by then. God orchestrated it for you to be alive to witness the year 2020 because glorious things will begin to happen in your life in the name of Jesus

In the medical field, the opticians call something a twenty-twenty vision. What does it mean? They set an object twenty feet to you. If you are able to see that image on the object, then your vision is great. We want to appreciate God Almighty who has spared our lives till today. He programmed and desired it to bring us into this year, not only bringing us in. He brought us hale and hearty with blessings and glory. This year is your year of blessings, promotion, advancement, peace, and happiness in the name of Jesus!

In Hebrews 2:7, that is where the Lord showed me when He gave me the revelation: "Thou madest him a little lower than the angels, thou crowneth him with glory and honor, and He set him over the works of thy hands." Every work of the hands of God will favor you this year. A thousand may fall at your right side and ten thousand at your left hand. It shall not come near you. And with only your eyes, you shall see it. Evil will not befall you in Jesus's mighty name.

It is not great men who changed the world but weak men in the hands of a great God. You are all in the hands of a great God. Your circumstances, your condition can never make God a failure. He has never failed from the foundation of the world up till now, and He can never fail forever. Now that you have turned to the Creator of heaven and earth, He will give you his glory and favor in the name of Jesus!

Glory means power without measure, tremendous power that cannot be withstood, the power that is more than the power of this world, the power that is more than principalities. Jesus Christ said that all powers in heaven and on earth have been given to you. He said that whatever you bind in this world is bound in heaven, and whatever you loosed in this world is loosed in heaven. Can you rise up and begin to lose something?

God is a God of glory. Ezekiel 10:4 states, "Then the Glory of the Lord went up from the Cherub and stood over the threshold of the house and the house was filled with the cloud, and the court was full of the brightness of the Lord's glory." You see how the glory of

God rose to bless and decorate the people of Israel, so also the glory of God will stand for you anywhere your name is being mentioned. Anywhere your documents are, anywhere you walk into this year, the glory of God will stand for you. The glory of God filled the tabernacle so much so people can touch it. That is how the Glory of God will fill your life this year. People will see you and say this can only be the glory of God. That is going to be your story in the name of Jesus! My God is so good.

In Revelation 5:12, see the glorious package Jesus put together and hand it over to you. It is ignorance that puts you in perpetual poverty. Jesus died for you to be enriched. Riches are not only in terms of money. Money is a by-product of blessing. Long life, good health, and old age are all embedded in the riches of Christ Jesus. You having no money today is no issue. The investment of heaven and the property God has invested for you. If you can open your eyes and see it, you will be dancing around for joy. He said to you, "Eyes have not seen, ears have not heard, it has never come to mind the good things I have in stock for people that love me" (1 Corinthians 2:9).

Revelation 5:12 says with a loud voice that worthy is the Lamb that was slain to receive *power*, *riches*, *wisdom*, *strength*, *honor*, *glory*, and *blessings*. Look at these sevenfold blessings that the Lord packaged together. What else are you looking for? When you have power, dynamic ability to cause changes, when you stand somewhere, witches and wizards begin to cry. I told you some time ago that you are not a Christian and a genuine born-again child of God if you fear witches and wizards. They are the ones to fear you because they recognize you, When you step in, they check out, They cannot molest you. Rather, you have dominion over them because God has given you absolute power over them.

Vision means *to see ahead*. Vision can be defined as the unfolding of the divine plan as it relates to you—that is, the plan God has for you. God is not a God of mistake. When He created you, He has you in His heart. That is why He declared in Jeremiah 1:5, "Before you were born I knew thee, before you were conceived in the womb and I have set you apart to be a prophet for the nation." So God has something on His mind. He has a plan for you in His heart before

He created you. And when He created you, He programmed you to be here at this particular time. He knows that in your journey of life, there will be troubles from your country of birth. He knows you will need certain things in your life's journey, He knows so He has set a plan for you to accomplish those things. It's only ignorance that makes you think as if He is not hearing your prayers. Destination is the work of God. Actualization is the work of man. Your part needs to be played for heaven to step into your case. If you want to drink orange juice, it doesn't matter how they love you at your favorite store. You still have to go get it from the store. So also is the plan that God has set for you on earth. The plan is ready with Him. That is why the Bible says, "Forever, oh Lord, thy word is settled in heaven." All the things you are going to need in life are already planned out and settled with God, but God is waiting for you to come back to Him and ask, "God, you created me for what reason and purpose?"

1. *Vision is divine insight into the plans God has for you.* When you can see ahead where God is taking you, what He is committing into your hands, that is what is called vision. Habakkuk 2:1–3 states, "I will stand upon my watch." Prophet Habakkuk was saying this: Why was he standing upon his watch? What does it mean to stand upon one's watch? If you refuse to stand upon your watch, God will be looking at you because every hero in the kingdom of God all stood upon their watch. So if you refuse to stand upon your watch, you can blame God for all you want or blame others. How do you stand upon your watch? You do it in fasting and prayers. "And set me upon the towers." How do you set yourself upon the towers? You set yourself upon the towers when you are isolated where there are no disturbances and distractions. You are by yourself upon the tower. No one else is with you where you can listen to God. "I will watch to see what He will say unto me." You are watching to see what the Lord will say unto you and what I will answer when He reproves me. What are you doing in this regard? You are preparing your heart. You are

preparing yourself. "And the Lord answered me and said write the vision." Any vision that the Lord is giving unto you, if you don't write it down, then God is not involved. God is a recordkeeper. Everything that transpires in the Old Testament, He also revealed it to them in the New Testament. Remember, when God brought Moses upon the mountain and gave him the Ten Commandments. When he came back, he broke the Ten Commandments. Do you remember what God told him? He said he should get himself ready to go back to the mountain and rewrite them because God wanted the record kept forever. God said, "Write it in your heart. Likewise, in our own case, God wants us to write our visions down. No matter how big or gigantic it may be, write it down. People might be looking down on you, but that has nothing to do with what God has for you. When He turns His glory to you, all the blessings will flow in a matter of minutes. The glory of God will begin to flow in your life in the name of Jesus! Alleluia to the Son of the living God!

"And the Lord answered me and said, write the vision." Every vision, whatever you want to accomplish this year, get a notebook and write them down. If you are not committed to your own life, how do you expect God to? When you get paid, you don't plan for it. The money will come and just go. If you have a plan, the first thing that will come to your mind is to fuel your plan and the agenda of God before you attend to any other needs. Program all your plans and work them out. You need to put yourself into it for God to help you. God will do it? He has done it, awaiting you to put yourself into it to accomplish it. Let this year be a year of accomplishment. God already told us, it's a year of Glory and honor. All you need to do is to have a set plan, a set goal that you can work on, and I see the Lord helping you out in the name of Jesus! Verse 3 states, "For the vision is yet for an appointed time, but at the end it shall speak and not lie." At the end of this year, I want to celebrate the glory of God in you. Your life can never remain the same. I don't know what you are looking for right now, but by the time we get to the end of this year, you won't be on the same spot. Regardless of what happened during the year, you will still come out triumphant.

Fasting and prayer are covenant doorways to the realm of empowerment. When you want the power of God to rest upon you so that you can take your inheritance amongst those that are sanctified, you need fasting. It has been medically proven that people that fast live longer. The fast in this regard has to be willingly done (Mathew 6:16), not forced. Set your mind at it. Program your mind to do it because, in the solution to your problem, you have a part to play. If you don't want to remain on the same spot, there's a need for you to watch. Let's begin this year by seeking the Lord. The Scriptures say that a wise son commits his way into the hands of his father in the morning. This is the morning of this year. Commit your way into the hands of your father.

2. You need to begin from the start. Start where you are. Everything in this life begins from scratch, The only thing that starts from the top is when you are digging a hole. But when you are building a house, you start from the foundation. So nothing of value begins from the top. If you want to start a business, and you are waiting till when you have a million dollars. No! You have to start from a little beginning. You don't want to start from the end. Only when you are digging a hole is the time you start from the top, and then you begin to go down gradually. Even when you are building a car, you start from the frame. A PhD man of today has to start from kindergarten. You cannot ask a toddler to start from college. Another thing I want you to do is to make particular use of your time. Don't allow time wasters to waste your time. If you have a friend who doesn't value time, it's better to stay away from such a friend. Set time for yourself in whatever you do. Time mat-

ters in your life. If you waste your time, you have wasted your opportunity. Jesus Christ commanded us in Matthew 6:16, "When you fast," meaning that fasting is a must, not if you fast. And He also commanded us in Matthew 6:16, "When you fast." He commanded us in 6:5–6, saying, 'When you pray." And He said to us in Matthew 17:21, "Howbeit this kind does not go out only by fasting and prayer." A member of this church was in a challenging situation. He went before the Lord in fasting and prayer, and God sent His minister to him to tell him the solution to his problem. During the time of fasting and prayer, God will deposit into you what will enhance your value in the name of Jesus. Remember, Moses fasted. Esther fasted. Daniel fasted. Even Jesus Christ, our Lord, fasted. I believe, with this glory, that God has shown me this year. I will join people. People will join me to celebrate your glory in the name of Jesus! Let us pray. Father, let your glory and honor be my identity this year in the name of Jesus!

01/12/2020
01/19/2020
Freedom in Christ

> Giving thanks unto the father, which hath made us meet to be partakers of the inheritance of the saints in light who hath delivered us from the power of darkness and hath translated us into the kingdom of his dear son in whom we have redemption through his blood, even the forgiveness of sins. (Colossians 1:12–14)

It is not enough when you come to the presence of God. but what is important is when you go home with the presence of God. When you come to church to meet the presence of God, that is not all of it. But when you are able to go back home with the presence of God in you, that is what is important. It is not possible for you to carry the presence of God anywhere and you are rejected. It is not possible for you to carry the spirit of God anywhere and you meet an untimely death. Neither is it possible for you to carry the presence of God anywhere and lose value or fail. Never. As you are going about your daily business with the presence of God, manifestations of His glory will show up in your life in the name of Jesus!

> For brethren ye have been called into liberty, only use not liberty for an occasion to the flesh, but by love serve one another. (Galatians 5:13)

There was delivered unto him the book of the prophet Isaiah and when he has opened the book he found the page where it was written, "'The spirit of the Lord is upon me because He has anointed me to preach the gospel to the poor. He has set me to heal the brokenhearted to preach deliverance to the captives, and recovering of sight to the blind, to set at liberty them that are bruised to preach the acceptable year of the Lord and he closed the book, and gave it again to the minister and sat down. And the eyes of all them that were in the synagogue were fastened on him. And he began to say unto them, This day is this scripture fulfilled in your ears." (Luke 4:17–21)

The quest for freedom is a theme found throughout the Bible from Genesis to Revelation. People desire freedom People love liberty. There is no one under the planet earth that doesn't want freedom. They want freedom from bareness, spiritual attack, pain, debt, sickness, everything evil, and everyone is looking for a means every day to be free. That is why we are running from one continent to another.

Right from the foundation of the world, people have been questing for freedom. By the third chapter of the book of the Lord, Genesis, Adam and Eve already lost their God-given freedom to the devil. And ever since they lost it, they had been searching everywhere for it. From that time forward, the perfect freedom God created in the garden of Eden was gone, and the long-term effect of it was both spiritual and physical. Every attempt had been made so that man can come back to that freedom. Men even sought God to see if He can return them to the original freedom He gave them at the beginning of the world.

In the first attempt, God gave men laws, which were not strong enough to give them the liberty they so much desired. Then He gave them prophets and prophetesses who did all the best they could. But their best wasn't enough to offer them the same kind of freedom God gave them in the foundation of the world. Lastly, Jesus Christ, the Son of the Living God, sees man wallowing in bondage and that the devil is tormenting mankind. They cannot raise their hands according to the measure of enjoyment God purposed for them from the inception. So Jesus now came to this world in a man form or in the flesh. He undertook the punishment God was looking for so that liberty can be given to people.

Alleluia! Man, in his best state, cannot meet the holiness requirements of God. There's nothing any man can do by himself to meet the demand of holiness required by God. There is no effort you can put in place. There is no amount of holiness you can show that is strong enough to meet the kind of holy life God wants us to live, but Jesus Christ, the Son of God, accepted to come to this world to go and die on the cross. So when he died on the cross, we died with Him. When they buried Him, we were buried with Him. When He rose up on the third day, we rose with Him. When He ascended into heaven, we ascended with Him. And right now, we are sitting at the right hand of God.

Jesus is now showing us how to be free. And that is the message I want to pass across to you today, how to be free. I want you to ask yourself, how can I be free from all the burden in this world? There is a way out. There is a way that witches, wizards, and familiar spirits cannot know. There is a place in destiny where you can sit in Jesus that all the principalities of this world cannot touch you because you are sitting far above them. They don't have access to you. They don't have power over you. In John 3:3, it states, "Verily I say unto thee, except a man be born again, he cannot see the kingdom of heaven." I pray I will be able to impart something that will not leave you in a hurry today.

Man is in three forms. Man is triplicate. We have the body, soul, and spirit, everything combined together in one. We are spirits having a soul, living in a body. And because of Adam and Eve, our bodies had been corrupted. We have sinned against God. Our bodies had adjusted to the life of sin (adamic nature). We enjoy sinning. We love every kind of sin because we are in the body. So we love everything that can bring enjoyment, fornication, lying, any kind that can bring pleasure to our body because we are alive in the body but dead in the spirit. The devil is the owner of the body, so everything that can make him happy is in the realm of the body. And those are the things we do and enjoy because we dwell in the body, so we can't do better. We don't know better than to do what pleases the devil in the body side. But when Jesus Christ came, He gave us His own life (gift of righteousness). Romans 5:17 states, "For if by one man's offence death reigned by one; much more they which receive abundance of grace and of the gift of righteousness shall reign in life by one Jesus Christ" And how did He give us His life? It's when you come and you hear the good news, believe the good news, accept the good news. When you receive that word, Jesus will come to you and give you a seed of the spirit, a little tiny seed just like a corn seed. He will deposit it in your spirit. This is called the spirit of adoption. Romans 8:15–16 states, "For ye have not received the spirit of bondage again to fear but ye have received the spirit of adoption whereby we cry Abba father. The Spirit itself beareth witness with our spirit, that we are the children of God." The spirit of adoption says that we are welcomed into God's family. The spirit of adoption God has deposited in you will begin to germinate gradually as you continue growing in your new nature. As you study the Bible, pray and fast. That little seed begins to sprout. It is just like when a man and a woman meet, and the man deposits just a little seed into the womb of the wife. You cannot tell immediately whether it is going to be a boy or a girl. But as the fetus develops, when the mother eats and drinks, the seed begins to get nourishment and grow. At a point after nine months, the baby is delivered. The outcome of that little seed that the man deposited into the womb is the baby, in the same vein Jesus Christ deposited a little seed into your spirit. And as you are praying and fasting, that little seed begins to get nourishment and grow. As the spirit is growing, the spirit of the devil in the body dies gradually because darkness and light cannot coexist. At this point, when the seed of the spirit of God is growing, that is when you can devote time to fasting and prayers. That is when you can evangelize. That is when you can resist the temptations of the devil because the spirit of the devil is terminated in you.

What is called self-discipline? It simply means abiding by a self-set rule. You might say to yourself in your room, "I will not lie again." When you say it to yourself, it's a little seed that you sow. And gradually, that seed begins to take hold of your life. The Bible calls you a fool when you set a rule for yourself and you cannot comply with it because you are still deceiving yourself. Let me tell you what the Bible says about that. Ecclesiastes 5:4 says, I'm not annoyed when someone deceives you but I'm angry with you when you deceive yourself.

Listen to me, this Spirit of God that has been deposited into you will give you freedom. That freedom is called freedom in Christ. Look at what Apostle Peter said in 1 Peter 1:23: "Being born again not of corruptible seed but by the incorruptible by the word of God." The corruptible seed is the seed of the flesh. It's the seed that draws you to do things that please the devil. The corruptible seed makes you lie, sleep around. The incorruptible seed in the above context is the word of God that has been preached. Romans 10:10 states, "For with heart man believes by righteousness, but with mouth confession is made unto salvation." Verse 17 states, "So then faith cometh by hearing and hearing by the word." You receive faith by hearing the word. Now if the Son sets you free, you are free indeed. How will the Son set you free? Jesus Christ sets you free. John 8:36 states, "If the Son therefore shall make you free, you are free indeed." Jesus Christ explains to us how the Son can make us free. Don't just claim, "I'm free." There are some things you need to do. When God gave me this revelation, and I made a mathematical expression out of it, I said 31+32=36. If you don't forget this expression today, it will make some positive changes in your life. Let's take a look at the thirty-first verse of John 8: "Then said Jesus to those Jews, which believe on Him, *if ye continue in my word.*" If you continue hearing the message from your pastor, if you continue studying the Bible, if you continue walking in the path of God, that is what Jesus is saying, "Then are ye my disciple." Verse 32 says, "And ye shall know the truth and the truth shall set you free." Listen to me. The little seed that Jesus deposited in your spirit is called the spirit of truth. The only thing that spirit is on the lookout for is the truth. When you begin to read the Bible by yourself, you will begin to know the truth because the devil has been feeding you with lies. You will come to realize the reason you should not follow other gods. Psalm 16:4 says, "The sorrow of people that follow other gods shall be multiplied." The devil might be enticing you, but the end result is sorrow. The Scriptures say, "Wine is a mockery and those that tarry by it are fools." You can like it or not, but that's what the Bible says. The Scriptures say, "Every fornicator and adulterer I will spit them out of my mouth." Revelation 3:16 states that it's either you are hot or you are cold. Lukewarmness is not permitted as a Bible standard. As you abide in the Word, the Bible is going to teach you the truth that is the work of that little seed Jesus deposited in you. Then verse 36 says, "If the Son therefore sets you free." Verse 31 says, "If you continue in my word, you will be my disciple." Verse 32 said that truth in my word will set you free. Now verse 36 says, "If now *the Son set you free*, the freedom is coming from the truth." And where is the truth coming from? It is coming from the Word. *So when you study the word, it will give you the truth, which in turn will set you free.*

That is the freedom in Christ Jesus! You are not your own. Somebody owns you, and that person bought you with a high price, which is His own blood. He went on the cross, received nails on His hands, and was crowned with thorns on His head. He was bruised, and the blood that was shed from His body was an identity for your price tag for God to reconcile with you. Jesus Christ had to die. He had to go to God and present Himself on the altar. He mentioned your name and mine that He shed His blood because of us. The resurrection is the receipt of the forgiveness of sin. Do you want all this to be in vain? Do you want Him to be ashamed of you in His Father's kingdom?

In closing, let me make this known to you that the number of years we are going to spend in this world is so minimal to what we are spending in eternity. The earthly things shouldn't be enough reasons for you to lose your heavenly home. Until you begin to fast and pray, that is when you are inviting God close to you. Jesus fasted forty days and nights for this same reason: to be able to walk with God while going about His earthly mission. In this same vein, why can't you do it? In the solution of your problem, you have a part to play. If your part is not played, then God is not committed because He is not a jester.

When I was growing up, at age twelve, if you were living with my mother, you had to fast and pray. You had to wake up at 3:00 a.m. every day when the bell went off for prayer. You have to suffer the flesh to nourish the spirit. You cannot be feeding the flesh continually, and your spirit dies gradually. When you fast, pray, and study the word, your spirit is growing to the extent that God begins to help you. He begins to open ways for you. What you think it's impossible, God will do it in a matter of seconds for you because your spirit has grown. This week, a member of my church told me that He saw Jesus walk into his house and told him that He has given him his request after some days of fasting and prayer.

Let us rise for prayer. Lift your hands toward heaven and say, "Father, I cannot do it by myself. I need strength from heaven because the scriptures say, for by strength shall no man prevail." Ask for an in-dwelling spirit. Ask for spirit upon. Father, Almighty God, according to what you sent me, I have delivered the message to your people. Father, according to the ability you gave me, I have given it out. God, you are mightier and stronger. Father, go into their mind and spirit and multiply these words in the name of Jesus! This seed that was sown today, let it germinate in their lives in the name of Jesus! Thank You, Lord, because you have answered this prayer. In Jesus's mighty name, we pray.

I want to give you an opportunity to accept Lord Jesus Christ as the Lord and Savior. Pray this prayer along:

> Lord Jesus, Lord Jesus, Lord Jesus,
> I ask for forgiveness of my sins.
> I accept Jesus as my Savior.
> I will follow Jesus as my Lord. Amen.

About the Author

The author is a vibrant and spirit-filled personality whom God has sent with the message of hope to liberate humankind from all forms of hopelessness. He is the pastor of Jerusalem Church of the Lord International in Maryland, USA. He is happily married to Christianah Ayeni and blessed with glorious children.

CPSIA information can be obtained
at www.ICGtesting.com
Printed in the USA
LVHW012004140723
752117LV00004B/746